The Little Blue Book on Police Ethics

The Little Blue Book on Police Ethics

By

Michael J. Lindsay

Xulon Press

Xulon Press
2301 Lucien Way #415
Maitland, FL 32751
407.339.4217
www.xulonpress.com

Contribution by: Denise N. Lindsay

Reviewed by D. N. Lindsay and Terrence R. Scherer
La Porte City Police Merit Commission Chief of Police (retired)

Paperback ISBN-13: 978-1-66286-512-1
Ebook ISBN-13: 978-1-66286-513-8

Dedication

This book is dedicated to all the fellow police officers in my life who have impressed me with their professionalism and dedication to duty. This book is written primarily to pass those attributes and perspectives along to the next generation of officers. Thank you for your examples.

Table of Content

Preface

My first goal for this preface is to reveal how this book is written so that we do not catch people off guard. I must admit that I have largely used a discussion-style approach for this book rather than a strict academic format. This will entail a kind of informal dialogue with a little humor mixed in. It will be somewhat like the very popular books Scott Kelby wrote on how to do Photoshop editing, a very technical subject. His books were so successful, I believe, because of his ability to make those technical processes easy for the average person to understand. I hope to do the same.

This relaxed style is, I believe, appreciated by the vast majority police officers. We will be quickly jumping into several complex areas that most police officers and their administrators have never really considered. Nevertheless, I very much want to stimulate real discussion in these areas! Why? Because most of these concepts are not absolute principles. Although there are some universals, what is proper and desirable concerning ethical standards for one department may not be proper for another. Thus, a discussion format.

I was also originally looking to provide a foreword for this book to help us get our discussion rolling. A foreword is usually written by some famous person who knows the author and has some knowledge of the subject. Because I do not know even one famous person, I scrapped that idea. Nonetheless, I do have a few thoughts for getting this discussion moving by referencing a famous person, now deceased, who has had a very strong influence in the writing of this book. He was universally recognized as someone who exhibited much worldly wisdom. Who might that be? King Solomon, of course! It is now obvious why I did not ask him to write the foreword for my book, although I am sure he would have agreed [humor]! His influence is, nevertheless, blended into every chapter and topic discussed in this work.

Among other things, I am hoping to generate some thought on several subjects that have not been adequately addressed in law enforcement *for many years now*! I will use King Solomon as my mentor for this process [not a bad personality for grabbing our attention]. He has some truly brilliant insight into these subjects, **truly brilliant**! For example, King Solomon realized that a civilization often repeats its worst mistakes simply because mankind refuses to study history. Solomon famously said, "***The thing that hath been, it is that which shall be; and that which is done is that which shall be done: and there is no new thing under the sun***," Eccl 1:9. We will see this thought repeatedly highlighted in the chapters to come.

Along this line, many admit that history seems to repeat itself, but notice that Solomon says something much more profound if we get into the details. He says "that" which is done is "that" which shall be done. He is claiming much more than a general truth. He is saying specifically, "that" which we have seen in history will be "that" which we will see again. I believe that this means when conditions in a society repeat, *very similar* future events will occur. This is very instructive for us, and we will use this often.

Many conditions today resemble the 1960s in some ways and the 1930s in other ways. Realizing this, the time seems ripe for some fundamental change. Although you may not yet understand why this is so, you will totally understand this by the end of the book. The truth is that the iron is hot, and we practitioners should be ready and prepared to strike. We are so blessed to be in the right place, at a right time. Hopefully, we will not miss too many of these opportunities.

Concerning this right-place and right-time thought, I must now also reveal a deep dark secret of mine. The right-place, right-time thought is really my motivation for writing this book because **I strongly believe that *the occupation of law enforcement is very close to becoming a true profession*!** Wow, am I glad that I got that off my chest! Well, you have now undoubtedly deduced that I also enjoy interjecting an occasional waggish [snarky] comment [although not necessarily skillful] into this *very dry* subject. Although such an approach tends to negate any scholarly sophistication that I might try to project [even if I were capable of that], I nevertheless realize that most police officers and police administrators really do not like reading scholarly works.

Along this line, those of us who have been involved in police basic training for many decades know that we do not refer to our function as "teaching" as I will do in the paragraphs below. We are, more accurately, labeled as instructors since we typically use the adult instructional model and adult learning principles rather than the pedagogy model for "teaching" youngsters who know practically nothing about a subject. Nevertheless, using the pedagogy approach for *this area of instruction* is now undoubtedly a better approach for police ethics training because it builds from ground-zero, so to speak. Consequently, this is the approach we will take in this book.

The statement about needing to start from ground zero is not a derogatory statement towards our incoming students but a reflection of the system from which these students emerge. I say this as their condition upon arrival at the academy, especially in recent years, has been and is still substantially below what most would expect for their entry level knowledge in those areas. In this book, I will repeatedly use the word "teach" because there is no longer a strong foundation upon which to build. Students now have very little education or background in civics, U.S. history, government, or Constitutional law, and practically no education whatsoever in comparative government, world history, or morals and ethics, even if they are college graduates.

As for our subject-in-chief, I began inserting some morals and ethics training into the very first class I was assigned those many years ago when I started teaching at the central police academy in Indiana. This block of instruction had a small section dedicated to law enforcement history, and it was into that class that I inserted this material. This, however, amounted to less than one hour. Not much! In years to come, that class on law enforcement history was one of the first to get cut when a new subject was added to the curriculum. I always felt like I was in a constant battle to reclaim an hour or two for my morals and ethics teachings because I thought these so crucial. My insertion of this material into that training was not a belief that ethics was a critical part of a historical presentation but that it was extremely important, was not presented elsewhere, and could logically be included in a history class.

I began instructing this block of classes in 1986. Most students were pretty well prepared in those days for handling the academy curriculum. By the mid-1990s, I realized that I needed to start "teaching" the basics of U.S. government because many students were arriving at the academy without enough of a foundation to even understand what I was attempting to convey in other classes. By 2006, I found that I needed to add even more material to that block of classes—again, starting from ground-zero—on morals, ethics, and professionalism.

I find that being able to generate a concept of professional ethics for American police officers generally will require what some call a substantial appreciation of our basic American ethos, specifically the concepts of "We the People" and "All Men Are Created Equal," as well as "… they are endowed by their Creator with certain inalienable rights," i.e., Constitutional standards, American history, etc.

Even though this book's title, *The Little Blue Book of Police Ethics*, reveals the real goal of this book, I find that a true examination of police professional ethics absolutely requires an awareness of morals and professionalism. Professionalism, in turn, needs a general acceptance of what a professional law enforcement service should look like. Personal ethics without morals and occupational standards is impossible.

This realization exposes the need for a broad examination of many related topics. This is not the perspective from which most police ethics training is approached today. What we will label in this book as "occupational police ethics"—don't take a bribe, don't plant evidence, don't lie under oath or in a report, don't steal at a burglary scene, don't arrest without "probable cause," and always be there for your partner—is taught in nearly all basic training academies but is *not* what we will be discussing here.

This complex topic of professional ethics is virtually untouched by academies and totally missing in departmental in-service training today. I do not mean to scare my readers when I use the term "complex." What I mean is that the subject matter we will cover is broad and intertwined, not that it takes an IQ of 160 or higher to grasp it. You will, hopefully, get a sense of this complexity even before completing this preface.

The fact that the ethical foundations upon which our American officers are trained is and should be substantially different and higher than the standards upon which police officers in China, Russia, North Korea, or Iran are trained. The occupational standards of *don't take a bribe* or *don't lie under oath* very well may be taught in China or Iran at their basic training academies, but we need better. As we mentioned in the second paragraph of this preface, all police organizations worldwide are not the same. We will also find that this is true even with departments in the same county or state.

Because new recruits now have very little background in what the Constitution requires, I found it necessary to address that area right from the very first week of recruit training. I would ask a new class why police act in this or that way when confronted with a particular type of situation. Typically, no one knew (or they were still too afraid to say anything). I would then answer my own questions with a repetitive stock answer: "*Because the Constitution says so*!" I have had officers who graduated from the academy in the 1990s come up to me as recently as last year and say that they remember me repeatedly using that phraseology until the entire class would recite it, in unison, after every such question. I, unfortunately, had to use that exhortation right up to the time I retired to impress students with the importance of adhering to Constitutional requirements. My point here is that one can have students quickly recall important ethical principles decades after instruction if done right.

Transitioning occupational police officers to true professionals will require an inspection 1) into what it means to have a true profession—whether that is a medical, legal, or law enforcement profession—and 2) upon which moral principles the professional standards will be based. Those two discussions encompass the entire scope of this book.

I do not want to burden our preface discussion with a lot of my personal experiences, but I have one final one that is worthwhile for justifying this claimed need for ethics training and for getting us started. I remember being required to take a class on "professional responsibility" for the education degree I was pursuing in my early college career. This course basically asked the question (for an entire semester) *what is a profession*? I later took a class on world ethics—examining philosophies like hedonism, utilitarianism, secular humanism, and the like—because it was one of only a few classes that was available to satisfy a degree requirement at my regional campus.

Surprisingly, I later found that when I switched to a criminal justice major, I was not required to have anything like those classes. In the promotion schools I have presented since my retirement, I have asked each class how many took a world ethics class or a professional responsibility class as part of a requirement for their degree. Many of those students were ranking officers and most had degrees. Less than one-quarter had ever taken such a class.

Being a "senior" veteran staff member at the academy, I had the distinction of having lived through the 1960s while being an eager criminal justice student and the 1970s while being a young passionate officer. Because of this experience, I now notice many of the same issues resurfacing today as had previously surfaced in those early days of my career. I must say that with all the time and money invested in those days in the President's Commission on Law Enforcement Standards and Training and in college tuition reimbursement programs, very little has transitioned into modern day policies or training that has helped law enforcement deal with our current crises. Other than what I have termed "occupational ethics," a broader examination of the subjects of morals, ethics, virtue, character, chivalry, and "right-thinking" was *even then* left primarily to the college educators. How is that working out today [oh my, I got a little snarky again]?

Nonetheless, these reimbursement programs were many-layered and pretty successful at getting officers into college. These programs were often sponsored by individual police departments, and such programs progressed right up through several federal agencies including the Law Enforcement Assistance Administration (LEAA) and the Veterans' Administration. That era (the 1960s and 1970s) saw the first great push towards professionalism for the police services. Prior to that, there was a rather meager step in that direction, although short lived, during the Great Depression. Those with college degrees applied for police department positions because those were some of the few jobs available, but that quickly waned when WW II hit. Younger police officers were drafted out of the police services and older officers found that they could make a hugely better living working within the defense-production segment of the country.

After I returned to civilian life in the mid-1970s, I remember local officers getting a college tuition reimbursement from their city police department, from the LEAA, *and* from the VA if they had prior military service, or from all three. This was a real step up from previous years not only in rewarding these officers with a little boost in pay but also in attaining a higher percentage of police officers with college degrees. As budgets again got tighter—as they always do—these reimbursement programs disappeared.

Today, there are very few tuition-reimbursement programs available to officers, and universities are loathed to require any type of true ethical training for graduation. In decades prior to the 1960s, nearly all citizens received some foundations in ethics and morals from church teachings and Bible reading, and through high school or college courses. Not so today! Consequently, new officers now arrive at the academy with virtually no background in these subjects whatsoever. Thus, this book! ❖

Introduction

Many have found fault with our education system today—which "indoctrinates" students into a far-left mindset rather than laying the foundations for the more traditional educational goals of our society—but I must admit that I, too, am going to attempt an indoctrination through this book. I believe one must have a certain doctrinal underpinning to become a truly outstanding police officer. There needs to be a core support system. Many departments today are engaged in a constant cycle of basic police officer training because they cannot hold officers for twenty years. A strong professional system, like the stout legs on a table, will help support a department's officers and supervisors in chaotic times and can actually *allow them to flourish*! Even an ornately carved banquet table without legs is just a set of floor planks. The same can be said of a police organization.

My presentation here will be mechanical as well as doctrinal, conversational as well as expository. It will be mechanical in that we must first know how a profession is structured in order to build a professional organization, but this examination must also be doctrinal in that we must instill virtuous thought processes and correct the very flawed worldview that truth, virtue, and character are whatever an individual thinks those are. Our discussions will not attempt a comprehensive examination of those ideals or of individual philosophies like hedonism, utilitarianism, Marxism, etc., but it will make officers aware of the views that can be used, ***or that should be absolutely avoided***, in the practical world of law enforcement.

This book will include an examination of why this ethical training is important today as well as what will likely occur in the very near future that will demand these changes. As abstract and bizarre as our discussion of likely future events may initially seem, by the end of Chapter 1, the reader will have a solid grounding in what to expect and why instilling a solid professional set of standards is so important.

In presenting these things, we will use stories and examples which I have actually heard, witnessed or experienced because most officers relate better to real-world teachings and because this really is a discussion. This is not meant to convert this book into my personal journal but to provide relevant examples. I have already used a few of my stories in the preface. When many of these things happened, they struck me at the time as being great teaching tools and lessons. These will be experiences new officers will likely have when they progress far enough through their careers. So, besides real-world examples, what will be my method for presenting this complex subject?

In short, we will first examine the structural requirements of a true profession. We will then move into a discussion of the individual virtues (honor, valor, integrity, etc.) required for a true professional. Finally, we will identify which worldviews (real world manifestations) are beneficial for a true profession, and why certain worldviews like Marxism and socialism are just plain bad for our occupation and our society.

I will then present a few recommendations for moving us towards our goals, but the majority of critical issues identified in this book will be left on the table for our current generation of officers and administrators to ponder and solve. This is, after all, an introductory discussion. This approach—leaving much of this material for further discussion—is how I can keep this work: *The* ***Little*** *Blue Book on Police Ethics*. It will be up to this and perhaps the next generation, using this information, to push us over the line, *if they will*!

Each chapter in this book is designed to be a stand-alone (future) study, even though that material intertwines with the material in other chapters and progresses in complexity. Consequently, there is some minor repeating of the ethical principles from chapter to chapter. This is not a repeat of the full discussion, however, and is not, therefore, burdensome. Overall brevity is a major objective in this work. When this restatement of ethical principles happens, there is also a reference to the original chapter for the convenience of the reader. Similarly, for brevity purposes, I will occasionally use acronyms—but not often—after fully identifying those the first time they appear in the text.

I will also use the gender convention, for brevity, of simply saying "he" rather than "he or she," or "him" rather than saying "him or her" or other modern labels in this gender-confused world. I will generally use the more informal and conversational first-person pronoun of "I" rather than the detached editorial "we" or the third person so often used in academic papers. "I" do not need to be a "them" or a "those." I am just me! [There, you now have a good sample of my lowbrow levity.] Will I offend some with this? Undoubtedly! I would ask my readers to consider that perhaps some inept, snarky humor is probably better than no humor at all with these dry and very dry topics. I know that this will not sit well with some, but I suspect that it will not offend veteran police officers in the least.

Likewise, my vocabulary will be that of the common man. I really want working class officers to refer to these principles and this book many times in the years to come. Consequently, this entire process, Chapter 1 through Chapter 14, will be presented with a light touch, with some humor, and without, hopefully, anyone thinking this book is a dry academic or doom-and-gloom presentation, a realm into which it could easily slide. The truth is that I consider law enforcement to be entering an era in which we find ourselves at the right place to ensure many positive changes.

I truly hope my observations will provide a few insights for the officers and administrators who are and will be charged with keeping the peace within our magnificent republic. Officers have many high hurdles in front of them today. Having now revealed some of these, let us get started with our examinations. ❖

Chapter 1

Why Now?

(Why Is This Book Critical for Law Enforcement Today?)

The author of any book, manual, or article always wants to answer this foundational question: Why is this work important? Authors rarely create a manuscript that they think has no relevance for their current time. In fact, many authors' core motivation is a belief that whatever they have to say will be very helpful, if not crucial, for their day. That is even true for novelists to a certain degree. The author must think that some thread within that novel will hook an interest within the current population.

I, too, possess this utilitarian belief for this book. In fact, I think the time for this work has truly arrived, heralded by the 2020 riots, BLM, Antifa, the push for socialism, the "Defund the Police" movement and all of the current anti-American efforts for abolishing the electoral college, changing the structure of the Senate, packing the Supreme Court, and creating new states out of Washington, D.C. and Puerto Rico.

In this book, we will be touching the foundational issues of why we should now begin to stress this type of ethical training, when we in law enforcement (for many decades) have only provided what we have labeled in the preface of this book as "police occupational ethics"—i.e., do not take a bribe, do not plant evidence, etc. Those, of course, are all good admonitions, but they are, as mentioned, very limited and very mechanical. What happens when an officer is confronted by another ethical question—like enforcing an obviously unconstitutional decree or forcibly confining citizens in an internment camp without a court order—not directly addressed with those rather limited examples? Does that officer have the moral experience upon which to draw a virtuous course of action? And even more foundational, can an officer ever hope to attempt this if that officer has no idea what the virtues are?

So, let us first think about *the why*. Why is today different than the last two hundred years? Why is real ethics training now crucial for what will likely be happening in our society very soon and what will those events be?

There certainly could be a book or even a series of books written on just this, but we will refine this question down to specifically what we need. In a nutshell, officers in the future are likely to experience what many officers did in the 1960s and early 1970s with the race riots, flag burnings, draft resistance, Vietnam demonstrations, and social upheavals of those days. Officers today are, nevertheless, also likely to experience many more things that the 1960s officers did not experience, including "Defund the Police," Antifa, Black Lives Matter, onerous and unconstitutional decrees, autonomous zones, school board disturbances, internment (anti-vaxxer) camps, the suspension of the writ of habeas corpus, "January 6th" type demonstrations, Sharia law, vaccine passports, and perhaps even a declaration of war or martial law.

Officers and administrators in the 1960s were caught off guard by all of those new challenges, but those officers and administrators in the later 1960s and early 1970s got much better at handling those situations with experience. Unfortunately, *none* of our current officers or administrators have had to handle anything like those emergencies. The question then is: Are any of the laundry list of events mentioned above likely to happen within the next few years? If so, should we be training *proactively* rather than relying on our usual slow-to-materialize and questionable reactive responses?

Some History

Although rarely used in any planning effort, history is a great resource for planning. We have already mentioned that King Solomon thought history an important *and precise* element in planning. If his earthly reign was any indicator, he was nothing but successful in dominating other kingdoms, accumulating wealth, and building a spectacular empire. He stumbled several times when dealing with the moral and spiritual realms, but that is another story. Noting what happened historically probably should be an important element in our planning for such events.

The police response to the manifestations of our current political issues can go largely in two directions. The police can do very little preparation for these mentioned confrontations, or law enforcement can begin moving towards becoming the professional organization that was envisioned at the end of the 1960s when the 1967 President's Commission on Law Enforcement and the Administration of Justice produced the seminal work, *The Challenge of Crime in a Free Society.*

This major document, largely forgotten today, outlined many things that were viewed as solutions for those days of race riots and burnings, Vietnam War demonstrations, and the like. Many of these "solutions" were actually tried. These were mostly the thoughts of the "Left," codified into that document, as a blueprint for the police going forward. Things such as abandoning uniforms for blazers and slacks were thought to present the police in a more friendly light. What was immediately discovered was that the police were still required to get into the gutter to make arrests no matter how nice-looking their outfits were. Other solutions were also found to be totally impractical like dividing a department into two to three status and authority levels somewhat like the military does with the officer corps and enlisted men.

There were, however, other aspects of this new approach that were never brought to fruition but *would have had enduring benefits*! One such thought was instilling a truly professional attitude within the occupation as well as creating professional standards for practitioners. Unfortunately, imparting these ethical attributes were largely left to the colleges and universities of the day. That made for a huge disconnect. What we now know is that the colleges and universities could not have been a worse choice for this task. What this undertaking *really needed* was a close examination of the philosophical views and foundations within the Judeo-Christian ethic *by law enforcement* itself. This, of course, includes an examination of a few Christian ideals, which colleges were loathed to present in those days, even as they are now.

So, why do we identify this as the one really important element of all of those Commission standards (several of those Commission standards books were nearly an inch thick)? This is simply because this is the one that has become so critically important today. Law enforcement, by design and structure, is the *status quo* component for our society, the stabilizer. We will soon recognize, in discussing the material in these chapters, that this anchor function is oh so important. These two opposite forces—chaotic change vs. stability—are so divergent that one is always at war with the other. The crucial thought here is that if law enforcement is to be the stabilizer, shouldn't it have a stabilizing set of standards within it?

As for those opposing forces, the concept of *Defund the Police* is the opposite of *Let's Make our Police Better*. U.S. police organizations are now, unfortunately, entering a no-win period in our history. But even this has positive elements to it. Today in my home state of Indiana—like in the 1960s—a huge appropriation was approved to add to and upgrade the Academy facilities, the first since 1992. There is also a proposal for increasing the number of Academy staff members to help handle all that is occurring in society. I have already noted the old saying: Strike while the iron is hot. Has anyone in law enforcement even noticed that the iron is now really hot?

The two big "whys" of this chapter—why is ethics training critical now and why are all of these things happening to the police (and society) now—will be the center of our discussion for the remainder of this chapter. There will be a few issues that some readers will consider bizarre, but please bear with me here. I think all will fall into place by the end of the chapter. We have much to examine.

The How of the Why

The truth is that we now know—from our 2020 experiences—that there are governors and mayors who are more than willing to establish an overbearing, tyrannical environment within this country that can easily perpetuate an image of "police oppression." Whether police organizations again play into this view or will (for the first time in history) establish a set of true professional standards—that elevates the profession above this unseemly stereotype—will not only make a huge difference in how the profession is viewed in the future but will also possibly influence whether America is worth salvaging.

Are police organizations ready for this new approach? I think so. I recently presented a couple of police promotional schools. I was pleased with what I found. Here is a short explanation of what transpired.

The Times, They Are a Changing: A couple of years ago, I had agreed to create a promotion school for a particular Indiana police department. I started the design process in January of 2020, and I formulated a rather typical curriculum. When I saw what was happening in March of that year, I called the Merit Commission for that city and asked if I could redesign the course and infuse a number of classes that would anticipate and prepare officers for what they would likely see in the upcoming months.

They, at that time, thought nothing peculiar about my request, and they gave me the go-ahead so I redesigned the course and included classes discussing civil disturbances, riots, burnings, and draconian decrees. All of these things happened much faster than even I anticipated. By the time the school was presented in October, several officers were amazed that I could have anticipated these things. Life had changed hugely from January to October of 2020. None of the anticipations on my part were quite as prophetic or mystical as it may have seemed, however. I had been a college student in the 1960s when *over 100 cities* burned in America, and I was an MP in the early 1970s when I saw, first hand, how quickly riotous situations can develop. None of those things were novel to me in 2020, nor would they be for anyone else who had started a law enforcement career back then.

In January of 2021, I was called by another department to create a promotion school for that department. I presented the same proviso as part of my proposal, i.e., that I would want to incorporate a number of classes that would prepare officers for what they would likely see in the coming year. I was attempting to reach a little further into the future with that course. That course, among other things, focused on many patriotic themes, virtue and worldview training, and establishing an in-service curriculum for training in First and Second Amendment law. We also talked extensively about their coming "1938 Moment" which we will discuss in some detail in Chapter 9.

That 2021 class relied heavily on discussion and officer input through a roundtable format. I think officers are ready for these ethical discussions simply because their involvement was so pronounced in those classes. This book has been designed to act more as a facilitator at a roundtable discussion than as an absolute how-to authority. Consequently, it is written in a nontechnical, conversational format. Sorry about the sidetrack, but this seemed a good place to emphasize that format explanation. Back to our promotion school.

As the graduates of that promotion school moved into the final portion of that year and then into the next, they recognized many of those 1st Amendment infringements occurring on a regular basis. From the Presidential inauguration in January of 2021 to December of that year, we Americans witnessed a huge change in our American governmental system. From rule by executive orders, through our Afghanistan withdrawal, to draconian OSHA requirements, to a socialistic mindset that almost instantly got citizens to depend on the government for their income, our country *was transformed*! The question started to be posed—never before thought possible—as to whether America would even survive as we had known it.

The Next Question, How Did I Know?

The next question that comes to mind is how did I know to design these courses in those ways? As hocus-pocus as this process seems, it is not at all mystical other than a good chunk of this comes from Bible prophecy, and the other, bigger part, comes from just watching current events develop via *non-legacy* media outlets. On this second matter, I would like to stress that if department administrators rely only on the mainstream media for their news today, they will always—and I mean *always*—be badly misinformed, unprepared, and well behind the curve on all developing issues. ***I cannot emphasize this enough***!

In every one of those classes, I asked how many knew who Klaus Schwab is and what are the goals of the *World Economic Forum* (WEF)? Not one student had heard of either of these entities, ***NOT ONE***! Many of those students were ranking officers. More on this in Chapter 10, "History as Our Schoolmaster."

Finding Better News Outlets (this is an important one)

Surprisingly, I find that the religious news outlets, although prejudiced in certain ways, are great news sources. These outlets tell you *right up front* that their news is from "a Catholic perspective" or whatever other perspective they use, all of which are a lot closer to the truth than any of the mainstream outlets are. I would recommend CBN (Christian Broadcasting Network) as a pretty good national news reporting source, and EWTN (Eternal Word Television Network) as a very good—Catholic-themed—international source.

I would also recommend administrators monitor at least one "edgy" news source, like *The Epoch Times* or *Project Veritas*. We have an excellent source for finding one or more of these outlets right here in Indiana through *Citizen Free Press*, which is based near Bloomington, IN. This source provides a handy listing of many other such sources on their internet homepage. I would hope that I never have another class in which my students or administrators (who are supposed to be preparing officers to perform in the future) have no idea who Klaus Schwab is or what those one-world organizations profess.

Using Actual News: Now more specifically, how did I know—through watching how things were actually developing—that the reaction to the pandemic would be so extreme, uniform, and fast to manifest throughout the world in the weeks immediately after March of 2020? Well, the radical Left badly needed and wanted a crisis. Members of *The World Economic Forum* (WEF) said repeatedly that they should "never let a good crisis go to waste" or similar verbiage, in the years immediately before the pandemic.

The WEF also said, just before the pandemic, that when this happens, it will be a very "*narrow window*" of opportunity. Knowing that, it did not take an anointed prophet to anticipate that those draconian measures would happen very fast, with much intensity, worldwide! And, that certainly proved true! Anyone who had monitored the "proper" news outlets would have known this.

Those law enforcement leaders who still do not know what the *World Economic Forum* (WEF) is and supports will continue to be *very much* out of the loop in the future. These nefarious actors are central! Again, why did everything seem to happen in such a coordinated, lightning-fast manner across the entire world? Just do a little research into the *Forum of Young Global Leaders*, a sister program with the WEF, and that mystery will totally disappear.

The Biblical Element: I mentioned that I pay attention to Bible prophecy to alert me to which developing trends are important and which are not. Talking about Bible prophecy makes many people *very* uncomfortable, so I will, consequently, not ask my readers to look up one passage of prophecy. I have already done that for them. Likewise, I will not attempt to get anyone to believe those passages. Nevertheless, I will mention those references—if you are interested—when I have relied heavily upon them.

My 2021 School and Future Events – "That Will Never Happen, Will It?"

When I designed my 2021 promotional school, I realized that people would likely say, "Oh, I doubt if that would ever happen." But this sentiment is what was actually expressed just before the pandemic surfaced in March of 2020. Does anybody remember the claim, "Two weeks to flatten the curve?" This is the same thing that was said just before our leaders imposed draconian lockdowns and decrees that totally destroyed the economy. It is the same thing that was said about the tyrannies that surfaced after January of 2021 that no one thought could ever happen here in America. And, it will be what people say concerning what I will reveal a little later in Chapters 8-10. You decide if any of these could happen in the future, viewing these things *now* from the perspective of the last two years.

Matching Events, After the Fact, to Prophecy –

I also realize that my readers may largely evaluate me as being unbelievably arrogant thinking I can prophesy the future. Let me immediately say that I do not claim anything like this. I readily admit that I cannot prophesy nor do I even attempt to predict. What I do is notice developing events and then compare them to biblical prophecy to see if these will likely develop into major important trends. This is an after-the-fact examination, not a prediction. To get a better feel for this process, notice where I talk about Matthew 24, in a few paragraphs from now.

All I am hoping to accomplish by this chapter, and book, is for this discussion to stimulate some thought and further discussion. It will be up to every administrator to evaluate what to do with this information. If current events, for instance, look like conflicts may develop between certain groups (say the police and certain demonstrators in Portland, as an example) and we get one or two of these, and Matthew 24:7 says that such group-to-group conflicts will be a *major part* of the latter days, then it might be reasonable, when these begin to happen, to anticipate some such future conflicts will occur (perhaps even riots). As they say, this is not rocket science.

Now here is the really mystical part of this process [this is me being snarky again]. If I see that we are going to have extended riots and burnings, I might make a few recommendations in such a promotion school that some crowd control and riot training should perhaps be considered for the future. Profound, huh! Such a thought is hardly an epiphany, but surprisingly very few police departments or academies are now training in these areas. Why not?

When I entered the military, we had riot training in my basic training course. I also received riot training in my MP School, in my Correctional Specialist School, and then at an in-service training at my permanent duty station. I also received additional riot training in my first civilian police academy. This was because we in law enforcement became much more competent about addressing those things after the turbulent 1960s manifested with such intensity. Might history be a good teacher [me being snarky again]?

I believe having a knowledge of what is coming is not only important but perhaps even critical because of so many new chaotic areas and groups that are surfacing today. This is just a part of what it means to have a professional cadre of officers. Establishing a professional organization goes hand-in-glove with developing ethical officers who will be called upon to handle all of these chaotic events in the future.

What Will Happen Next – Looking a Little Further Down the Road

Upon making these statements, several additional "why" questions naturally surface. We should not only further discuss *why* ethics is so important today, but also *why* these things are happening. Can we stop them, and how do I come up with these "tin hat" predictions? What are my sources? Do I have a track record of any accuracy in my beliefs? I will start with this last question first because it presents a threshold for belief.

Well, noting how closely the training classes designed for the 2020 and 2021 schools matched what was actually developing in society at that time is perhaps the best validation for using this process, i.e., watching developing events (current news) and seeing how those compare to biblical pronouncements. I know this sounds like a very ambiguous protocol and does not yet instill much confidence in this process, so I will give a few examples of what I used to help design the 2020 and the 2021 schools.

Using Matthew 24

One has only to notice what Matthew 24 proclaims to get a pretty clear idea of what the latter days will look like. The disciples asked Jesus directly what the end-time signs would be. He related, among other things, that nation would come against nation at the very start of the process. Back when this was written, nation meant ethnic or people group, i.e., people group against people group. Boy, has that happened! When I first started noticing this, it occurred to me that we in law enforcement should start thinking about riot training, crowd control, Stockholm Syndrome, suicide recognition, emergency preparedness, and op-plans for a number of areas. Pretty mystical, huh [perhaps too snarky].

This Bible chapter also says that there would be a huge amount of deception occurring at that time.[1] Check and double check. That led me to recommend alternative news sources to the officers in those schools. Have we ever seen so much lying, even among our governmental leaders? Then in verse 12, it says that lawlessness would abound. That led me to suspect that even our governmental leaders would ignore our Constitutional protections, including the really important First Amendment freedoms. Did we elect our leaders to protect our Constitutional freedoms or to become absolute despotic tyrants at the first excuse? Check, check and triple check. This led to including a number of topics in the 2021 course having to do with ethics, morals and worldviews and recommending in-service classes on our First and Second Amendments.

Matthew 24:6 also reveals that there will be wars and rumors of wars. That "rumors of wars" wording seemed very strange to me until February of 2022 when we saw the threat of Russia invading Ukraine. Would they invade or not? Are they withdrawing or actually increasing their forces? Are those war games or actual preparations for an invasion? Will America and Britain evacuate their embassies? American said that Russia would invade in two days. That deadline came and went, twice. Ukraine then chastised America and Britain for their war-mongering dialogue. What a strange time in which we live. Yes, *rumors* abounded. Now we see some truly serious things developing in the Middle East. Will Afghanistan become a breeding ground for terrorists? Will Iran get the bomb? We know of the threats Iran routinely makes against Israel and the U.S., the little Satan and the big Satan.

Matthew also predicts pestilence in the lead-up years. We have now seen two pretty dramatic years of that, COVID and the aftermath. Check, check, how many checks is that? Never mind. So, what is left to happen? Not much. Verse 8 says that these will be like birth pangs,[2] meaning that these will become more intense and frequent (sorry, no return to the old normal), and verse 6 says that these are the lead-up signs. Think about President Biden's inauguration day for a good picture of the birth pangs. How many executive orders did he sign that day? Verse 9 is then a transition verse. It starts with the word "then." Things mentioned in the previous verses announce the preludes, but *then* verse 9 and beyond announce what will happen in the Tribulation, what some call the "Great Reset" (for this term, do an Internet search on the WEF).

But how do we even know that today is the time period spoken of in Matthew 24? Well, other prophecies say that this generation, meaning the generation from the reestablishment of Israel in May of 1948, will see *all* of these things come to pass.[3] The Bible in Psalms says that a generation is from 70-80 years.[4] That means we are getting towards the end of that time period, and so all of those remaining prophecies must come to pass pretty quickly. Even Matthew 24:15 announces what is undoubtedly identified by scholars as a mid-tribulation event. So that is the timeline!

Now I am aware that very few believe in the Bible today, even including professing Millennial and Gen Z "Christians." Some surveys say that only 6% of Americans now have a biblical worldview, which of course includes professing Christians.[5] Wow, that was a surprise to me! This same survey revealed that 30% of senior pastors believe that someone can get to heaven by good works. Even fewer believe, I suspect, in the literal fulfilment of Bible prophecy, *but I do*, and that is what gives me guidance when I see something starting to develop in our world. I do not predict, I just observe. So far, I feel like this has proved to be a highly reliable process.

I will not drone on about prophecy other than to say, for the benefit of police administrators, that the next really big thing for law enforcement to realize is that the old "normal" will not ever be returning as so many Americans and officers have hoped. Perhaps we actually need to prepare and train for this new paradigm. Many won't! But if we are forever on a new course, what do we in law enforcement need to notice specifically for the next few years? Luckily, you are reading this book. So, read on!

The New Normal

I realized that within one year of that 2021 promotion school, some states in America would actually propose internment camps, like Australia has constructed, i.e., "Democrats File New Bill Authorizing 'Strike Force' to Imprison Unjabbed Families: 'Our Internment Camps Are Ready'" [state of Washington].[6] The police will, of course, be charged with making the apprehensions to fill these camps if these come into existence, a grim prospect!

I realized, even then, that more draconian decrees would be proclaimed in certain states in 2021, creating an even wider political divide. Banning the non-compliant from stores, restaurants, and most public areas would become common even though studies are consistently showing—although not reported in the mainstream media—that omicron has a very, very low fatality rate, especially among the very young. Other studies show that lockdowns are ineffective and that even the vaccinated can transmit the virus.[7] Of course, the police would be called upon to enforce these tyrannical decrees as well.

Christian churches and related church programs and facilities will be particularly targeted across the world. The police, of course, will be called upon to arrest local pastors and priests, and those friends and family attending those services, all of which have now happened around the world and in our neighboring Canada (as of the writing of this book) and are beginning to happen here in America. Again, very sad, especially for the police.

How should officers handle these draconian, unconstitutional, and immoral decrees? We previously mentioned that we talked extensively in that 2021 promotional school about what we labeled as their "***1938 Moment***" (The Night of Broken Glass).[8] We will explore this in a subsequent chapter in some detail. All of the above are extensions from what we have already seen. So, what can we identify as likely new trends materializing in the next couple of years?

Future Trends

What are the more distant future trends for which law enforcement agencies need to prepare? Well, it seems pretty certain that the split in how conservative states and liberal states handle governance will continue to widen, and the federal government will place considerable pressure on conservative states, organizations, and people in the coming years, meaning creating an even wider divide within the country. Nearly half (48%) of Democratic voters think federal and state governments should be able to fine *or* ***imprison*** anti-vaxxers.[9] Another "WOW" as far as I am concerned!

Since the coronavirus pandemic has waned slightly, at least for now, and the U.S. Supreme Court has already declared several really draconian federal rules unconstitutional and a number of injunctions have been placed on several other federal rules by lower courts, it is likely the Left's efforts will shift, at least temporarily, to international issues over which the federal courts and Congress have very little jurisdiction or power but will, believe it or not, have many ramifications for local police.

What is this indirect approach going to look like? It will involve big, BIG spending within the areas of foreign relations, e.g., vaccines for everyone on earth, abortions financed internationally, and especially support for foreign militaries. It will involve international supply chains, primarily meaning fertilizer and crop production, meaning shortages and high prices at the grocery store. It will involve very expensive treaties like the Iran nuclear treaty, climate change, and the Green New Deal. When our local law enforcement administrators say, "Good, none of those things have anything to do with local law enforcement," I will need to disagree strongly.

National Politics Really Does Impact Local Police: One of the early signs of the latter days will be that food shortages will begin to manifest all over the world as will substantial inflation.[10] This will largely be the result of wars, see Revelation 6:3-8. All of this will lead to trashing the economy worldwide. What does that mean for local law enforcement? It means civil disorders, riots, flash looting, and burnings. When food shelves are empty and prices are sky high for gasoline and other commodities, there ***will be*** a reaction in the communities. This is already beginning. Because of the war in Ukraine, wheat cannot get out to feed the people in Africa and other famine-sensitive regions.

Many Millennials and Gen Z citizens are already dissatisfied with our system. Recall Portland's autonomous zone and the five miles of Minneapolis business district burned to the ground. This will mean continued calls for major changes in our governmental structure which will include more welfare-like programs, i.e., socialism. That will result in an even weaker economy. It will mean civil disturbances when these changes do not happen quickly enough. Millennials will be the voting majority from this point on and many of them already think socialism is the better form of government. Conservatives, of course, will be attempting to hold on to what they have. That is what conservatives do!

Some of the real impacts for law enforcement will be that cities and towns will be able to afford fewer and fewer officers during these financial crises. This also means that cities will only be able to purchase half the gasoline needed to run normal patrol shifts. It means that the remaining officers will need a *strong moral foundation* to see the benefit of what they do (this is also a major reason for writing this book).

It means, among other things, preparing to train officers and administrators in crisis and emergency management protocols and community involvement procedures. It means developing op-plans for when the demand surfaces to enforce immoral, unethical, brutal, and unconstitutional decrees. It means developing some *best practices* for crowd control, riot maneuvers, gas dispersal, staffing internment camps, and dealing with an officer's "1938 Moment." If that is not enough to give you some direction, I could continue. But, none of those things could ever happen, could they [you got it, snarky]?

Many Officers Onboard

The design of the 2020 and 2021 schools were "prophecy influenced" but focused around actual developing events. Somewhat surprising to this author, as mentioned, was how receptive those officers were immediately after the initial 2020 shock-and-awe events occurred. They were not only receptive, but truly participated heavily in all of those prophecy-influenced classes and discussions.

Even though none of the officers were prophecy literate, ***not one***, I think the thing that made the schools so successful was that all of these officers had a sixth-sense, an innate awareness, an intuition, that those things were coming. I think they all had a realization that neither the riots nor the pandemic was going to be a flash in the pan. They knew that these were just the first in a line of catastrophes that were going to continue along with other natural disasters and that we citizens will not experience any real return to a traditional "normal."

They saw, first hand, how our governmental officials reacted, and they immediately noticed—because they are trained to be attuned to Constitutional protections—that these officials totally ignored any and all constitutional protections having to do with First Amendment rights or limitations. I think they all realized into what an untenable position that these draconian decrees place them and their profession.

Consequently, talking about concepts like chivalry, virtue, professional structure, suspension of the writ of habeas corpus, internment camps, emergency decrees, and martial law—that would have seemed very strange for a promotion school just one or two years earlier—were all received well and generated much discussion.

I think officers are very aware that they are entering uncharted waters, and they are hungry for answers and ways to prepare. That is what this little book on ethics is designed to supply. This book could in fact be a supplemental source of information for those schools. It is a source to help get officers and administrators going in the right direction. It provides no absolute solution, but instead, a number of foundations upon which to build for our uncertain future.

My hope is that this book will help fortress officers against all of these future pressures by creating mutual support mechanisms through colleagues and departments, by recognizing that they are doing necessary and noble work, and by understanding how to avoid immoral acts, authoritarian responses and unconstitutional procedures while involved in these sure-to-come situations. Having identified these many initial issues, the question becomes: HOW DO officers handle these challenges? Well, fasten your seatbelt, hold onto your hat, and read on [oops, snarky again]! ❖

---

[1] Matthew 24:4, deception

[2] The New American Standard Edition uses the words "birth pangs." Other versions use the word "sorrows."

[3] Matthew 24:34, this generation shall not pass away

[4] Psalm 90:10, a generation is 70-80 years

[5] "Only 6% Of Americans Believe Biblical Worldview, Barna Survey Reveals" https://www.christianitydaily.com/articles/11996/20210527/only-6-percent-of-americans-believe-biblical-worldview-barna-survey-reveals-family-research-council.htm

[6] "Democrats File New Bill Authorizing 'Strike Force' to Imprison Unjabbed Families: 'Our Internment Camps Are Ready'" [state of Washington] https://apps.leg.wa.gov/WAC/default.aspx?cite=246-100-040

[7] "New York declares COVID state of emergency as governments across globe race omicron variant"

[8] "Night of Broken Glass," November 9, 1938 https://www.history.com/topics/holocaust/kristallnacht

[9] COVID-19: Democratic Voters Support Harsh Measurer Against Unvaccinated. [1/12/2022] https://www.rasmussenreports.com/public_content/politics/partner_surveys/jan_2022/covid_19_democratic_voters_support_harsh_measures_against_unvaccinated

[10] Revelation 6:6-8, inflation and food shortage (also known as the Four Horsemen of the Apocalypse)

Chapter 2

Finding Bedrock for a Foundation

This chapter will provide the big picture for our discussions, the 30,000-foot view for accomplishing a massive task: the police professionalization process. We need this overview to get a sense of what we must accomplish in each of the subsequent chapters and why that chapter is important. We start here with finding some solid "bedrock" onto which we can pour our ethical foundations, but we will quickly find that all other chapters of this book are also built upon this bedrock, both figuratively and actually.

Finding really solid bedrock sounds relatively easy, but it is perhaps the most difficult part of this entire process. The building analogy that we will use throughout this book will take us into a step-by-step process for uncovering some moral truths (our bedrock principles), establishing a set of ethical standards (pouring our foundations), and identifying our structure and critical virtues (building the superstructure of a true profession, in particular, *our* professional structure). Even though we will be using a "building process" analogy, some of this will be accomplished using a reverse-engineering progression. This is simply because many people today do not have the background to recognize what we will call our moral imperatives. So, in some areas, we will reveal the obvious and accepted, and then work backwards.

Well, if we are working backwards in some areas, how will we progress through this book? This sounds really complicated. It is not. We will first discuss those areas that are the most familiar to many and that are the easiest to understand. Our book's progress will move us from easy to complex. Certain things are readily apparent in our 21st Century world. Others take a little work to uncover and understand. We will expand into those more difficult and complex areas, some of which will actually take us backward compared to a true building progression.

Consequently, we may talk about some superstructure issues and next discuss some foundational issues. If we will be jumping back and forth, why even use this building model? Using this building analogy is still very worthwhile because it *reveals the relationships* between components, e.g., bedrock to foundation, foundation to sill plate, sill plate to superstructure, superstructure to façades and finishing details. By the time we get to the really complex areas, we will be well prepared to handle all of those issues. This chapter will, again, contain some of my experiences that illustrate those things. Most veteran officers have like experiences that they can draw upon, but new officers do not.

Again, A Little History

When I first started in law enforcement as an MP (military policeman) in 1971, I had taken my first criminal justice class a few years earlier, at the height of the civil unrest of the 1960s. It was at that point I began to transition my career goals from teaching (an education degree) to law enforcement. Why does that have anything to do with the subject of ethics? In short, there were few situations in which one could get a broader perspective on the subject of ethics than being a college student in the 1960s and then a policeman in a rigid military system shortly thereafter. At my ETS (discharge) from the Army, I heard several career MPs say that they had no desire to enter civilian law enforcement as those officers were losing their authority on nearly a daily basis.

This seemed a true statement when viewing the number of Supreme Court decisions in those days concerning police protocols. Under Chief Justice Earl Warren, the court had decided to "federalize" criminal justice standards like it did the abortion issue. Surprisingly, those decisions were a great foundation for starting the professionalization process for the police services. Miranda Warnings, the Exclusionary Rule, the silver platter principle, and many other criminal justice decisions (as wrong as these were Constitutionally) provided a great foundation for police procedures that was badly needed at that time. They did not quite approach an "ethics" level for police decision-making, but they at least presented a unified system nationwide. That unified system largely started us towards creating a more professional, ethical occupation.

This was important because we, as an occupational group, did not yet have the discipline generally needed to take those first steps on our own in such a difficult time. We will begin our discussions here by doing the same thing: pouring a foundation! We will identify several characteristics concerning foundations even before talking about what should be used for our bedrock because these foundational attributes are more familiar to the general public, and easier to understand, than the attributes of a good (solid) bedrock.

A Foundation

As previously mentioned, I had to take a professional responsibility class and a world ethics class early in my college career. I thought these classes, at the time, to be a horrendous waste of time. I now recognize that these were some of the most valuable classes of my career. Who knew that as I became a practitioner within the law enforcement system that I would be referring to these moral teachings on nearly a daily basis?

In my second year of pursuing an education degree, I received my draft notice, and I decided it was time to make my career change. I signed up to become an MP. Again, besides the above, why is any of this important for any discussion on ethics (as I am sure all of my readers are now asking)? Well, when I began instructing full-time at the Indiana Law Enforcement Academy in 1986, my exposure to that broad range of attitudes and philosophies became very beneficial. I had operated for years in both extremes: the highly liberal philosophies of the 1960s' college campus environment and the extremely conservative environment of a policeman within a military service. Both exposures have served me well, and both have convinced me of the need for interjecting an ***independent set*** of professional standards into a basic officer's educational process. Why are those independent standards necessary?

One very important reason is that these standards help keep officers on an even keel in turbulent times. No matter what point in history we find ourselves, officers can become extremists ***within the law*** on both ends of the spectrum. Police can and do occasionally use these extremes as a club for *political* purposes. These are what I label as ethical abuses. Think: our current FBI! Of course, many officers would say anything that is allowed, even if it gets substantially into gray areas, is always okay. We will be talking about discretion extensively a little later on, but for now, let us realize that every grand swing of politics has seen abuses in this area. So, do we need some additional mileposts beyond what the Constitution and current police procedure provide? I contend, absolutely yes, if we are going to become true professionals.

In the days of my early career, this political bludgeon involved developing and using the "conspiracy" laws to create a "dragnet" for pulling everyone into legal liability with even a passing acquaintance to the communist party, the SDS (Students for a Democratic Society), the Weather Underground, the Black Panthers and other such groups even if those persons did not participate in the actual criminal act. The term "dragnet" is not used much anymore because of its undesirable connotations, but it was the label attached to a television series and a movie and, in fact, to exactly what was happening then. Those were the days shortly after the Joe McCarthy era. That should draw a picture.

Pursuing communist sympathizers was a full-time career for some law enforcement officers in those days.

Today, it is the other political extreme that controls the narrative. Today, it is the "hate laws," created by those on the Left, that seek to punish severely all who do not have a "politically correct" mindset. This by necessity, in their view, is to get and keep the upper hand. These hate-laws are designed to literally attack America as we knew her for the past 200-plus years, especially the Christian element. Of course, this effort is, today, worldwide. In Finland—as this book is being written—there is a minister who was what we would call the Secretary of the Interior for that country who is now being tried under their "hate laws" for publicly reading Bible verses and producing a pamphlet, way back in the early 2000s, quoting Bible verses on marriage.

As hate crimes take on an increasingly broad perspective, and they are, can America be far behind? Will reading Bible verses in unison, in church, led by a pastor, be viewed as committing a hate-crime in the future here? This is almost certain.

Because of these extremes, the need for good *independent* ethical standards for law enforcement becomes even more apparent. Unless we pass laws to cover every possible police encounter, an impossibility, creating true ethical standards seems the logical answer. Today especially, I see a need for ethical standards to counteract those expanding hate philosophies as many new officers now bring no moral or ethical foundations whatsoever to their new profession. Those moral belief systems, however, are the "bedrock" principles for building a just society *AND* a professional law enforcement system, i.e., a police ethic.

Circling Back to Bedrock –

We have strayed a little here by discussing ethical foundations when this chapter is supposed to be about finding bedrock. That is because most can relate somewhat to having standards for police conduct (a foundation for our police ethics) even if they do not really understand where these standards come from or how these standards should be constructed (the bedrock principles). So, let us now take a step backward. The old saying goes that one who places his foundation on sand will have his house swept away during the first hard rain. Without some bedrock principles, it is difficult to even pour a foundation.

This naturally brings up the question of what should we then use as our bedrock principles, a question a little more difficult for modern man to discern than the fact that police organizations should have some standards by which to operate. In our politically divisive society today, it is even difficult to get anyone from one political extreme to acknowledge any good whatsoever coming from the other side. We instinctively know that a conservative philosophy is better for maintaining the *status quo*. That is the very nature of the concept itself, i.e., to "conserve" a principle, concept or philosophy, but that is not the only worthwhile worldview out there, and we should not think that it is, regardless of what the current political system says.

Along this line of reasoning, it is also true that if no change had ever happened, we would still be living in caves. I, for one, like my comfortable house, big car, open society, and freedoms. Frederick Douglass once said, "**Those who profess to favor freedom, and yet deprecate agitation, are men who want crops without plowing up the ground**." He, of course, was alive during our country's most extreme time of internal dissent, the American Civil War.

So, my point for this little discussion is that using political or academic or emotional or hedonistic criteria for our "bedrock" principles is like pouring our foundation on sand. We need an unchanging standard for our bedrock. All of these other standards—political, academic, and so forth—are destined to destruction. So, where can we find the rock-solid principles that we need for building a strong house?

A Real Problem Has Developed in the 21st Century

Two people could, *ad infinitum*, argue about what the benefits of a college education are in today's society, but most would agree that the current indoctrination process used in most colleges today—and now in many high schools and grade schools as well—is not conducive to stability. Nearly all college students today have been propagandized into believing that "truth" and moral standards are whatever they think they are. There is no absolute standard. No wonder we cannot decide what is right and what is wrong. Consequently, I will leave such debates to the academics, and I will look for a *stable and unchanging* standard upon which to pour my foundation.

Rather than involve ourselves with those tedious arguments and details, I will suggest, without further comment, that using the standard that was used prior to the 1960s for the entire two centuries of our republic is what we should use today. It was, and largely still is, what is known as the Judeo-Christian worldview. More on worldviews later in this book.

Finding True Bedrock: Timeless vs. Changeable, Granite vs. Sand

The Judeo-Christian worldview says that there is an unchanging definition of "truth" and an unchanging set of moral standards. Why unchanging? Because these are set and given by God rather than by man. These moral standards do not fluctuate from generation to generation nor from era to era, no matter what mankind is facing at any particular moment in history. Although it sounds counterintuitive, officers who subscribe to this view will actually find freedom in this approach.

I have now mentioned the terms morals and ethics without providing any background on these terms. We should, consequently, supply at least an introductory definition for these concepts as well as how they fit within our "building terms," as used in this book. Defining these terms first is necessary for understanding the rest of this book. We will get into much more detail on all of these terms and concepts a little later in this book. For now, here are a few important terms.

Bedrock; Our Moral Laws –

These are the divine moral teachings which do not change. These include the Noahide and Mosaic laws including the Ten Commandments. They include a few biblical principles on character as well. They are the constant element in our discussion, sometimes referred to as "truth." Because they do not change, they are the solid sub-foundation upon which we will build our entire profession.

Much Confusion: A year or so back, I heard my pastor use the terms morals and ethics in an inverted way to which I would have used them for that particular explanation. Upon arriving back home, I went immediately to several dictionaries thinking I had misused these terms. To my surprise, I found that every dictionary defined morals by using the term ethics, and every dictionary defined ethics using the term morals. I later found that this circular definition problem occurs with a number of virtue terms as well. Even the term virtue has a few circular or confusing definitions. One older definition of virtue is strength, which many would not have guessed. Because of this, we will be using very specific definitions for all these terms for our purposes even though many in society use these terms interchangeably. In our examples, morals are given by God and ethics are manmade.

Foundations; Our Ethical Standards –

These are our ethical mandates, our most fundamental *manmade* principles for a society; they are a human interpretation of the moral laws. These are poured upon the bedrock morals that God establishes. They conform to the curves and creases of the bedrock. These (the ethical standards) are universally accepted throughout a culture. More specifically, these implement the moral standards. One definition of **ethics**, in the Merriam-Webster dictionary, is: ***the science of morals as it endeavors to divide men into the good and bad.***

In the American historical experience, these foundations have manifested in what we call the Judeo-Christian ethos or worldview. These are the things that *stem* from our moral underpinnings. "Professional ethics" is *a specific adaptation* of those (Judeo-Christian) foundations. They are one more step removed from our moral bedrock but not as changeable as the culture's mores and norms. Ethics can apply to a particular subgroup, like a profession (see our Sill Plate discussion, below). Hopefully, you can now see what I am attempting to do. I am attempting to show a layering here in a way that relates our ethics examination to our "building analogy," i.e., a moral bedrock, under a societal ethos, under a professional ethic, under a culture's current norms, mores, pop attitudes, and politics. Simple, huh?

These Are All Connected: The changeable social norms and mores of a particular group or society (part of the superstructure of our building analogy) always play into how any profession operates within a nation, society, or subculture. We will make an argument that there must be some higher ethical standards within any profession, to be a profession, that should control behavior in that profession even if the cultural norms change substantially.

This indicates that a profession could stand in opposition to a current set of norms. ***This concept is important***! For instance, the medical profession could stand squarely against a governmental edict that everyone should get vaccinated. This may be because the "vaccine" has no long-term tests, does not have enough data to provide for "informed consent," has some counterindications, and has ingredients that are kept secret by the manufacturer.

Nonetheless, there is no doubt that these societal norms influence behavior. As an example, imagine, as mentioned previously, a group of policemen from Iran or China or North Korea or even Russia coming to America and being hired here as policemen without any cultural indoctrination. What could possibly go wrong? [Okay, I will attempt to limit my snarky remarks as we get deeper into our examination, but this is very difficult for me.]

Using the medical profession as an example again, might the medical profession be influenced by a government very suddenly infusing billions of dollars into the health care systems—hospitals, clinics, and hospice centers—that makes these hospitals, clinics, and practitioners very profitable? One influences the other, for good **or** bad.

The Sill Plate –

We have now touched upon our foundations and bedrock principles. Let us now move up to the next level in our building analogy. The sill plate, as used in this book, is that which connects the foundation (our Judeo-Christian ethos) to the superstructure. In our analogy, this will be the "professional ethic" for a specific discipline, say law enforcement, for example.

A sill plate sits directly upon and is attached to the foundation, usually by huge bolts. It is perhaps the strongest component of the entire building. It does not derive its strength from the superstructure; the superstructure derives its strength largely from being attached to the sill plate. Are you seeing the analogy here? Consequently, when a hurricane or tornado hits a house, the superstructure may be totally destroyed, but the sill plate and foundation typically remain.

An *occupational* ethic, as previously identified, can include admonitions like: Don't take a bribe; don't plant evidence, don't lie on the witness stand, etc., and is really part of the superstructure. But the *professional ethic*, the sill plate, is more basic and incorporates some important principles, i.e., canons of conduct, like: *No officer will subject any citizen to an excessive use of force*; or *officers will remain alert so as not to violate a citizen's First Amendment protections*; or *all citizens will* *be treated equally, without any consideration of their race, color, national origin…* These are all man-created principles but typically reflect some foundational beliefs or bedrock teachings.

The Superstructure –

From here, we can start building our ethical superstructure: "Don't take a bribe," which is like the 2x6 framing in a house. It is also an extension, several steps removed, of a moral principle, like the commandment of *Thou shall not steal.* Taking a bribe is taking money one did not earn. "Don't plant evidence" comes directly from *Do not bear false witness.* Do you get the idea?

From here, we can build the architectural features of the house and install the ventilating, plumbing, and electrical systems, and then select the façade, paint color, roofing tile, etc. The ventilating and plumbing systems are our vision and mission statements and our department code of professional responsibility. Paint colors, and façades are our policies, work rules, op-plans, training goals, and directives. SOPs might be viewed as our home's hardware: door knobs, latches, window locks. These are the things that make day-to-day operation possible.

The superstructure is built above ground, for all to see. The heat ducts and all the things that make a superstructure habitable, functional, and desirable are incorporated within this part of our structure. This includes the placement of electric outlets that make appliances convenient, like a professional certification or licensing requirement makes decertification easier if not almost convenient. This includes the flashy part of the structure that typically impresses people.

A superstructure can be built in many different ways, using many different designs and styles, and employing many different façades. **Choosing one façade** over another can impact how well a particular building sells in the marketplace [there must be an analogy somewhere here; sorry, I said I would limit these remarks]. Nonetheless, these are the things that make the public believe they have a first-class police department, but that façade is really pretty superficial. Superficial does not, however, equal unimportant.

Façades typically sell a structure. By comparison, the foundation and sill plate must be done in one of only a couple of ways if these are to give the superstructure any real strength. Altering either of those can be very problematic for any superstructure. The variety of paint colors for a house, however, are almost unlimited. I think most can see my metaphor here.

A Really Big Problem for Law Enforcement

A current serious problem for law enforcement today is that we have a huge gap between our general code of ethics (our sill plate), and the façade of our profession (our SOPs, etc.) without having created much of a supporting structure in between the two.

More specifically, we have a generally accepted code of ethics—the International Association of Chiefs of Police (the IACP) Code of Ethics, for instance—but then have very little in place until we get down to our specific department SOPs. This would be similar to building a house with no furnace, only two electrical outlets, and walling 2x4s, seven feet on center. A look at other professions reveals our shortcomings in this area in rather dramatic fashion. Do we even have canons of conduct? How about a department code of ethics or peer-reviewed standards or a best practices committee, and so on?

Consequently, we have included these higher-level attributes like creating canons of conduct or developing virtues in officers within our building allegory so that we can make these complex issues a little easier to understand. These are all attributes that should be within the superstructure of our profession. These are what people notice, admire, and appreciate even though they may not be as important as a good foundation. In fact, these noticeable attributes may collapse rather quickly if there is not a good foundation, secured on solid bedrock, when the troubles begin. That is why we are again returning to the issue of morals and ethics in our next section in this overview.

Morals and Ethics

As you can see, we have already incorporated the concepts of morals and ethics into our building analogy. As for further defining these terms, we will keep this simple for now by just saying that we will use the term **morals** to mean those unchanging principles that God provides to man and **ethics** to be those manmade rules for society or for those particular groups within a society, like a profession, that stem from the unchanging morals.

One Standard Does Not Fit All: We have also defined what we call occupational ethics—e.g., do not take property from a burglary scene—as being something like the structural features of a house, but more accurately, they are very much a part of a ***particular*** profession. After all, doctors, accountants, and pharmacists (all professionals) do not typically have the opportunity to respond to burglary scenes, so they do not need a standard that says: "Do not take property from a burglary scene." What is our point here?

Each profession has its own set of professional ethics, many of these being very different from other professions. An established profession like medicine has many intermediate standards. A new profession, like law enforcement, has few intermediate standards. Henceforth, we will strongly make a case for law enforcement needing more intermediate standards than they presently have, especially for being able to handle all of the new challenges it will be facing in the years to come.

Many Ethical Standards – The Same Moral Imperative

As stated, professional ethics can be very different from group to group—and we will argue, from department to department—even if they stem from *the same moral commandment.*

Perhaps a better example is that an ethical standard for law enforcement may be that an officer will not point his weapon at anyone with the safety off unless this or that is present. This would stem from the moral rule that *thou shall not kill* (murder). An ethical standard for the medical profession could be quite different even though it stems from the same moral rule of thou shall not kill or murder. It might say something like: A doctor shall not perform an abortion past the 12th week of a fetus' development unless this or that is present. Here we have two ***very different*** ethical standards stemming from the same moral commandment, thou shall not murder.

When entering a time of great turbulence, it might even be desirable for ***each department*** to fill this huge gap rather than waiting for profession-wide intermediate standards at this time. Many local intermediate standards are like many laboratories conducting experiments on how best to handle these situations, much like our fifty-state nation. In fact, departments within the same state have different focuses that beg for different standards.

Pouring the Foundation – Extremes–Another Potential Problem: Having introduced all of those concepts for our consideration, let us now start our examination on how to pour a really strong foundation. Without a strong foundation, even a beautifully built or remodeled house will immediately start to settle and crack.

As mentioned earlier, neither political extreme has all the answers, and some important questions having to do with law enforcement are not even political, although many observers today will attempt to pound these perfectly round law enforcement pegs into some oddly shaped holes of ideology. Political ideology can become a real problem when attempting to develop a just set of professional standards.

An important "foundational" point that I would like all of my readers to ponder over the next several chapters—before we consider those concepts in real depth—is that if law enforcement *must* operate in this extreme political spectrum of making no arrests, for instance, in order to appease Antifa or the BLM, or being unthinking arrest-robots (zero-tolerance policies) to keep everything "fair," to satisfy some on the other side, we then, within law enforcement, should begin to realize that neither of these extremes is good, and we should avoid both.

Of course, people on each end of the spectrum will not like that. But, shouldn't we have a set of professional standards that are truly independent from those extreme political influences so that we have a demonstrable standard for not adopting either extreme in a crisis? Please ponder this before we arrive at Chapter 7. It is important!

Establishing The Standards; How To -

So, how do we actually establish these standards? At this point, we are not going to tell you (or your departments) what to put into those standards, only that you need them. We will get into content a little later in this book, but even at that time we will not be prescribing many absolutes. Our police administrators are bright people and can hammer these out for their departments.

When I say we should "***establish***" these professional ethics, what I mean here is ***to write these down***, publicize them to the officers, post them, include them in printed material and applications, announce them to the public, and reward them in annual employee evaluations and at Christmas parties and in media releases. This is the façade we show the public.

Discretion and Taking the Heat: One critical component to such standards is allowing for *a substantial degree of* ***discretion***. What we will soon see is that this is an important element with *any* true profession. Allowing some discretion will drive the "zero tolerance" people insane, but it is worthwhile. Written intermediate standards can, of course, totally eliminate discretion if written too tightly, but these standards can be a basis for making those discretionary decisions and can eliminate problems like singling out a protected group for excessive enforcement and arrests.

Nonetheless, there is nothing wrong with keying on a criminal organization. Criminals are not a protected minority. The problem comes, naturally, when a criminal organization is primarily also a protected group. What this means is that supervisors must be ready *to take the heat to a certain degree* [clever wording, sorry, I can't help myself] and to honestly adjudicate complaints from many sides. Well-written intermediate standards certainly assist in this! In fact, supervisors will find these invaluable when these confrontations occur.

And This is Just the Overview

I am sure, at this point, my readers are beginning to realize how complex this task will be. Be not afraid. Because this book is designed to begin with the easiest principles (starting in Chapter 3 and building towards the most complex) everyone will be ready to tackle all of those complex and scary concepts when we get to them because we have paved the way.

Two Perspectives: This chapter was tedious but necessary for us to have a foundation from which we can discuss the rest of the story. For the rest of this book, I will present this subject from two perspectives for simplicity's sake: one mechanical, the other behavioral. We will discuss the mechanical aspects of a profession first as this is the simpler of the two. So much for the overviews. It is now time to begin pouring a few foundations. ❖

Chapter 3

Pouring the Law Enforcement Foundation

We have mentioned that there is a biblical admonition to build your house on a rock and not on shifting sands. So too, with the building of a profession. Our previous discussions have revealed that for high-level police ethics to really exist requires professional structure and virtues. Both of these will be built upon our bedrock of moral imperatives.

Our discussion on building a professional structure requires establishing a few mechanical elements like an independent code of ethics along with canons of conduct, mission statements, etc. This first structural objective—having a code of ethics—has already been done for us, to a certain degree, by accepting the IACP Code of Ethics. This code, of course, could be supplemented or modified or replaced by a department, but the acceptance of that code provides a real shortcut for us. Thank you IACP!

The second major area—the character traits of practitioners—is a little more esoteric and difficult to discern. What virtues are required of a law enforcement professional? Who establishes those? How are those instilled? Are they ever modified? Who enforces them? We will address these critical questions starting in Chapter 7. For now, however, let us start by discussing these structural components.

The Structural (Mechanical) Components of a Profession

A dazzling superstructure of virtues and ideals must be built upon the ethics of the profession, which should be attached to the foundation of the society it serves, which hopefully, will be anchored upon the bedrock of truth. [Pretty intellectual, huh!]

Okay, let's get serious. Beyond these general analogies, we will not get overly tedious in using our building metaphors. You are probably sick of this already. Recognizing that there are also bolts that protrude through the sill plate and into the foundation or nails that attach the walls to the sill plate adds no real clarity for our purposes, but it certainly can infuse mind-numbing complications. Our building metaphor has already served its purpose even though we will continue to use it to a lesser degree for the remainder of this book, i.e., to show elemental relationships. One thing is built upon another. One component gives another strength and durability. This is what we are trying to demonstrate.

Digging Out the Mechanical Aspects of a Profession – Any Profession

We should examine a few of the concepts and terms used within a profession to distinguish a true profession from an ordinary job, occupation, skill, trade, craft, or art form. This is a good way to start our examination as it is pretty simple and obvious to most people that these terms, e.g., job, craft, profession, do not mean precisely the same thing. If there are elements that make a difference between these employment levels that seem worthwhile for elevating an occupation, like law enforcement, we should obviously strive to incorporate those elements into our criteria. Where we find overlaps between these terms and concepts (and there are several areas of overlap), we will assign a very specific definition to that term for our purposes.

An Important Observation: I often see real world events that I think at the time would make great teaching points. This is one of those. While instructing at the academy, I often asked a new class if law enforcement is a profession, or not? Typically, ninety percent or more of a class of 170 officers would raise their hands indicating that they believe law enforcement is a profession. This is not surprising. Everyone wants to think they are part of a noble undertaking.

I would then ask, "Why?" What is it that distinguishes a profession from an ordinary job or occupation? Why might a city police officer be classified as a professional when a city street department worker is not considered a professional level employee? Both employees work for the same mayor and receive their paychecks from the same legal entity. So, what is the difference? What are the elements that are necessary to have a true profession compared to an ordinary occupation? Upon asking these questions of a new basic class, I was always met with a deafening silence.

This idea of becoming part of a noble profession is strong in new police recruits, but the truth is that they have thought very little about this possibility. I then attempt to help them out a little. I ask them to think of what the recognized professions like medicine and law have. More specifically, what distinguishes a CPA from a bookkeeper? Is there a difference between a nurse practitioner and an LPN or a nursing assistant? What is the difference between a pharmacist and the clerk at a health food store?

It was always obvious to me that they had not (in their collective mind's eye) visualized their new occupation, perhaps their new profession, as being in the same league as these other professions. That is a shame because I think they were able to see, by the end of the hour, that law enforcement is not that far from becoming a true profession.

They Finally Get It: Once encouraged to do so, the elements needed to have a true profession like medicine started to flow. This thought process always began very slowly, like a little trickle of water rolling off a rock, but by the end of the hour, the ideas were flooding out like a tidal wave or tsunami crashing down a canyon after a dam bursts. In fact, a one-hour class was rarely long enough to discuss these suggestions. Those new students spouted ideas almost faster than I could write them on the chalkboard [yes, I still use a chalkboard, and no, I do not own a cellphone; can you say dinosaur].

By the end of that hour, we had typically identified a few virtue elements but many more mechanical elements necessary for a true profession. By the end of this chapter, we will also have identified and addressed a few of those important mechanical elements as well as revealed several different levels of employment that will get us started in our evaluations and give us a few insights into the professionalization process. This will also lead us into using this comparative approach—between law enforcement and a profession like medicine—to see what we have already accomplished and what we may need to develop a little further in the future. Most will be surprised by how far we have already come. Let's start by looking at some differing sophistication levels in employment.

Some Instructive Employment Levels

I have already mentioned the terms: job, occupation, skill, trade, craft, art form, and profession. How do these differ? We will use some fairly specific definitions. Along that line, the above terms are certainly not the only words associated with employment relationships, but these few terms are more than enough to get us started and to give us a perspective.

A Job: It seems to me that a job is employment (although the term is also used for non-employment situations) in which a person simply performs services for pay. This does not need to be the same type of service each day. I remember seeing the building contractors in Mesa, Arizona, pick up laborers every morning from a town square. Some days, those people would be helping with roofing. Other days they might help with drywalling. On other days, they would be pouring foundations. These were pretty much what most of us think of as "day-labor." At the end of the day, they would receive their pay, and the next day they could be doing something totally different.

An Occupation: An occupation seems to be somewhat similar to a job but perhaps focusing on a particular type of work or employment consistently, day after day. For instance, a salesperson at a clothing store generally does not have a real high level of technical expertise in the types of leather used in a particular type of shoe or in the cloth used in a fine suit, but he regularly sells suits, shirts or shoes. Because of this, he eventually develops a level of familiarity with suit design or certain types of cloth simply because he does this day after day. He is probably a good source on trending styles, durability of a certain kind of cloth and the like.

A Skill: A skill is usually thought of as an employment (although this term is also used often in non-employment situations) that requires a level of *manual competence above what a member of the public can do without some training and practice.* A welder is a skilled worker. One cannot walk into a welding shop and create strong welds on different types of metal without some specific knowledge and a lot of practice.

A Trade: A trade is generally thought of as an *organized group* of skilled workers who are represented by a trade organization. Originally, this word merely meant the business of buying, selling, or bartering but this has taken on additional meaning over the centuries. These "trade" organizations today often provide training to perpetuate and upgrade the trade. They may have entrance standards. Trades often act as unions for the skill group and represent that group to outside interests. Several recognized trades today include electricians, plumbers, and carpenters. In earlier times, these were known as guilds or leagues. These trades often designate (rank) competency levels within a skill, e.g., apprentice, journeyman, master.

A Craft: A craft is usually thought to be a skill that requires not only manual competence but also a degree of creativity (a mental process) that infuses an element of beauty or symmetry or another aesthetic element into the product. Craftsmen have a lot of discretion in how they design their products. Other workers—day-laborers clear up to master tradesmen (an electrician for instance)—have very little discretion in this area. Potters, wood carvers, macramé weavers, and the like are often viewed as having complete creative discretion with their products.

An Art form: An art form is a step up from a craft. An artist is someone who has advanced manual skills but also creates objects that involve *a high degree* of creativity (a mental process) in addition to the manual skills and technical knowledge necessary for that creation. A sculptor is an artist. From this definition, one might logically conclude that an artist is just someone who is higher on the "creativity" scale than a craftsman, but this also seems to include a higher level of mechanical skills as well. Shaping a soft clay pot seems less demanding than sculpting a full-sized statue of Zeus out of a block of marble. I once heard someone say (although I cannot find the source now) that a craftsman knows what he can create. An artist is never quite sure.

A Few Bogus Elements

As you have probably now noticed, there must be additional elements necessary to define a profession as we ascend this hierarchy of employments, from job through art form, but as always, there are also elements that some say are important but are really irrelevant. We very much need to sift out these bogus elements from the start. Having an association to represent the occupation (like a trade organization) is very important, but we can also get very bogged down with supposed elements that confuse this process. We need to identify these. Here are a few.

Separating the Wheat from the Chaff: A "professional" painter can be someone who paints houses or paints murals on a wall or paints portraits on a canvas or paints the ceiling of the Sistine Chapel. Not all of these obviously require the same skill level. Consequently, we will need to make some distinctions to determine what is needed for a true profession and what is obviously below that level. We will examine this span of talent in more detail shortly, but for professionalization purposes, let us just recognize that there is a difference between a house painter and Michelangelo. In short, we must learn to separate the wheat from the chaff, so to speak.

Professional vs. Amateur: Recognizing that we have stepped up from describing a day-laborer to an accomplished artist, and from a house painter to Michelangelo or Leonardo da Vinci, we can now use these distinctions to see what we must do, at the very foundational levels, to begin forming law enforcement into a true profession. In the examples above, a "professional" housepainter is obviously only a professional in the sense that he does that full-time as his paid employment rather than being a homeowner who paints his house every ten years or so. Does simply being paid for a task transform that person into being a professional?

Many False Criteria

Professional Sports: The term "false flags" has become a popular term today, but it does accurately describe a condition that leads people astray when considering what it takes to become a true professional. "Professional" golfers, basketball players and football players will not be included in our definition of a profession, even though they are full-time, highly skilled athletes in those occupations. They are not required to take an oath of fidelity to a code of ethics, and they are not required to adhere to a set of virtuous attributes (discussed in detail in Chapter 5). Likewise, these athletes also fall short of our definition in several other areas, like satisfying a "critical need within a society" and membership in a "professional organization," (also discussed in detail in Chapter 5). I know, I am getting ahead of myself.

Nonetheless, with those "professional" athletes, the term is more of a distinction between those who do that skill as full-time employment compared to those who do it as recreation or as a part-time semi-pro or as a highly talented amateur. Why do some people seem to place them in a "professional" status? I will make the suggestion that this might be because, more than just being employed full-time, they make so much money and are so skilled. We, especially in America, have always awarded an unofficial status to those who are very rich. We will discuss this in just a couple of paragraphs, but first, what about this skill issue?

Having Very High Skill Levels: This criterion is why I often use the term "true profession" throughout this book to highlight these distinctions. "Professional" basketball players certainly have attained a very high level of skill in what they do, like Michelangelo did in the art world. The competition for those high paying professional athletic jobs is intense, and so the high skill level required is no surprise. Nonetheless, the sense in which *we are using* the term professional designates more than just being highly skilled, as explained above, although one would expect a professional to be pretty skilled in a specialty after *years* of "practice," but this probably isn't the case for a *new* practitioner. So, is a high skill level a true criterion? Perhaps a minimum level is.

A High Wage Rate: So, if being paid—or not—is not a criterion for creating a true profession or being a professional, is having a certain wage level *within* a *recognized* profession, among other criteria, necessary? For instance, think about the difference between a medical doctor and a nursing assistant. Is a high pay rate *within* medicine considered a crucial element for that profession? Doctors generally earn a substantial wage. There is no doubt that because many professions are difficult to attain, they tend to be compensated at a higher wage rate. One is then tempted to look at medicine (a recognized profession) and others like broadcast news anchors, etc., and conclude that making a high wage might or must be an element for these occupations to be recognized as a true profession. Is a local newscaster not a professional because of a lower wage rate than the national newscaster?

Consider that although national news anchors make a substantial wage, there are local news reporters and anchors who are just scraping by but are very professional in the way they collect and report the news, perhaps even more so than our current national reporters and anchors. Is what those local reporters do any less important to a community? Speaking of *being needed* in the community, let's examine this criterion in combination with a high wage rate. More specifically, let's look at pastors, priests and law enforcement.

The Clergy: Along this line, most would say that a priest or pastor graduating a seminary and then being ordained satisfies the entrance requirements for participating in a profession (we will soon see that this was one of the original professions). This line of work is, in fact, where most of the terms and concepts used for a profession originated.

A few priests take a vow of poverty while others do not. Is a priest who takes a vow of poverty not a professional because he does not receive a regular wage even though he graduated from the same seminary as the priest who takes a salary? Both priests perform the same duties. In prior times, medical doctors did not make nearly the income they make in America today. In fact, in many developing countries, doctors work for low wages even today. Is an American doctor a true professional since his wage is high, while those other doctors are not because they make a much lower wage?

The Police Specialty – Are highly paid private police (working for large corporations) considered professionals but lower paid public police not considered professionals because they make less? Should big city officers be considered professionals and small-town officers—who generally make much less—not be considered professionals? You are probably tracking with me now even though there may still be that nagging feeling that most small-town officers are just kind of backwards, the

Barney Fife condition. Here again, this is human nature. Big always seems more impressive to us humans.

Along this line of thought, is the small-town officer's job any less critical to the community when there is an active shooter at the school? Do we expect less out of the small-town officer when the active shooter shows up? This *small* and *poor* perception plays on our collective minds as making these things less important. One gets a sense of how complex this discussion can become when factoring in human nature and the interplay of many elements, e.g., wage, criticality, competence, etc. This aspect of human nature if powerful. Here is a short example to bring this into sharp focus.

Several years ago, the Indiana Law Enforcement Academy (ILEA) participated in an officer exchange program. We had a police officer from Brazil visit our academy. He related to me that he was a licensed medical doctor who worked in his private practice every morning until about 1 p.m. He then changed into a uniform and worked the second shift as a policeman in his local community. He truly loved being a policeman, but could not afford to live on the wage given to officers in his small town. Among other points of our discussion, he mentioned that Brazil had five major language groups. He spoke a little of all five languages. If I were to use *only a wage criterion* to judge if this officer was a true professional, this officer would certainly be the most professional non-professional I had ever met. Or would that be a non-professional professional? [Boy, am I easily confused.]

I experienced a like situation when I was the marshal in a small town. I had a reserve deputy who really wanted to be a full-time policeman but could not afford the pay cut. He was a security policeman at one of the large steel mills in northwest Indiana and made nearly double the wage we offered. We were always jealous of those private police departments because they always had the newest radar and breath-test equipment and the best cars, and they always had more video and camera equipment than us and got the most in-service training.

Does Money Really Matter – Yes and no. Upon thinking along these lines, it is apparent that money is not a critical element for a profession, but it does play a strong indirect role in being able to hire those who are willing to accept these higher standards. One must be able to make a living. Unfortunately, the general public often has a sense that a high wage rate indicates a true professional from a non-professional. I presented this long-winded section to demonstrate this is NOT SO! **The reason I key on this is that the *real problem* here is not how the general public views this. *It is that incoming police officers also have this perspective*!** That is the real problem! Consequently, they often cannot view themselves as *ever* becoming true professionals. How sad!

Okay, I guess I have now beaten this issue to death, but it is an important one. It frames, in a couple of ways, *how new officers view themselves.*

More False Criteria That We Will Save for a Later Discussion: We will discover other criteria, like education, that the general public assumes are necessary parts of a true profession but are not. We will identify those as we proceed through this book. They are reserved for later discussions because they really fit with some of our more advanced considerations. Just to give you an idea of what we are saying here, we will again mention the areas of education and training. These are very important to all true professions but in a little different way than many think. For instance, is a college degree necessary for true professions?

If so, is a two-year college degree sufficient, or is a four-year college degree necessary? Is a post-graduate degree required? This supposed requirement surfaces because many professions require a college degree, and the public, therefore, assumes this is always necessary. Consequently, I will undoubtedly beat this topic to death in Chapter 6 as well, but it is critical to our examination of professionalism.

Although I may have droned on a bit too long on these false criteria, these distinctions are important for recognizing what we absolutely need and *what we don't.*

Ascending Levels of Employment – Does Law Enforcement Qualify?

Having identified some areas that do not qualify as necessary elements for a true profession, we must get back on track for the real reason for this chapter. We must now see if we in law enforcement qualify under those ascending areas of employment that we have already identified.

The Exclusive Manual Skills Requirement: Using those levels of employment, discussed above, law enforcement certainly satisfies the advanced and specialized manual skills requirement. We must demonstrate our ability to shoot a handgun and a long-gun to a high level of competence before we are allowed to graduate from an academy. We must exhibit many high-speed driving skills to the academy instructors. We must demonstrate how to restrain a typical arrestee without permanent injury to either the arrestee or to the officer. These and many others are "mechanical skills" that the general public *does not possess*, and therefore, ordinary citizens cannot step in to fill a vacancy when an officer calls in sick on any particular day.

As we also saw in our employment examples, having an organization to represent the profession, its members, and issues within the discipline is the next significant step up. Do we in law enforcement qualify there?

Having a Professional Organization: Trades, over the course of many centuries, have developed systems to represent those skill areas to the public and to improve and refine those skills including training, a rank system, membership (hiring) standards, and the like. They may even have behavior requirements. When you hear the terms apprentice printer or master mechanic, specific thoughts come to mind.

The medical profession certainly satisfies the "**professional organization**" criteria in which their organizations provide recognized standards and training. Along this line of thought, who would want someone performing brain surgery on their dearest relative if that surgeon had not satisfied the recognized standards of the profession for that area, ***even if*** that person was a medical school graduate. Internships and fellowships within the medical profession satisfy some of these advanced requirements. So, some advanced standards and requirements seem very worthwhile and even necessary. These are most easily accomplished through a professional organization. Obviously, at least one professional organization is then necessary for a true profession that operates in a critical area for society.

Does law enforcement satisfy this organizational requirement? In almost every aspect and state, yes. If not exclusively through our own standards, then through standards set by state licensing boards like POST (police officer standards and training) commissions and other such agencies. In some states, these standards are extensive (with "best practices" committees and the like) but in other states, not so much so. Along this line, one such weak component in this area that we will discuss shortly is establishing canons of conduct for our departments.

The Creative Problem-Solving Requirement: Stepping up to the highest tier in our employment level example, we recognize that crafts and art forms require a creative element for each item produced. I think we can also readily acknowledge that there is a creative element needed in every call handled by a police officer. No two calls are the same, even if they are both domestic violence calls. It is just a fact that we cannot train specifically for every situation to which an officer might be called. This reveals that training in the general disciplines, like ethics and discretion, are important for professions generally but especially for the police profession.

We have already mentioned the need for a great deal of discretion in this occupation. That certainly is a component in all true professions. Professional discretion is just another way of saying **creative-solution-thinking**. One domestic abuse case may result in a referral to a counsellor whereas another such call may result in the arrest of everybody at the scene.

We have already mentioned a frightening scenario in which an active shooter may arrive at a small-town grade school where the local police department is small or very small. We asked the rhetorical question: is the police mission any less important when this happens with a small, poorly paid police department? Taking this active shooter scenario to the next logical step, do we need a scene commander who can form a bunch of problem-solving cognitions almost immediately? Obviously, we do! It would seem that this creative "art element" of the job is inherent with the policing function.

If our commander is not a creative-solution-thinker, or he freezes, really bad things have happened. This also shows how canons of conduct, op-plans, and policies are—when our commander or officers are not creative-solution-thinkers—hugely important. Op-plans and canons of conduct are all like training in that they tell an officer what to do in that type of situation.

For now, however, we have established that law enforcement already has satisfied these first three critical elements for a true profession: specialized manual skills, being part of a professional organization, and creative thinking abilities. Nevertheless, there are others.

Most know what a calling, vows, a vocation, a covenant, canons of conduct, a code of ethics, a creed, a career, and the like mean generally, but most, including new policemen, have not thought about what those mean specifically to the profession. We will begin looking at these in our next chapter. ❖

Chapter 4

Critical Elements for Any Profession

We could generate a hugely long discussion here on all of the important elements and sub-elements of a profession which would be wholly inappropriate for the condensed examination of this subject that we promised in this manual, this ***Little** Blue Book of Police Ethics*. This tiny work is focused on identification of these issues, not on a full examination of each. Those reading this book can dig deeper if they see fit. Those extended topics might be a worthwhile excursion for a college class on police professionalism or an in-service training, but not for this book. So, for now, we are going to reduce this examination down to the "brass tacks," the essential elements, of a profession.

As mentioned, students at the academy would begin to recognize the important elements necessary to create a true profession once they started identifying the elements that doctors, lawyers and CPAs seem to have in their professions. The class would then start firing back ideas like a minimum educational level, specialized training, a code of ethics, licensing or certification, continuing education, and an approved organization to represent the profession. Once nudged in the right direction, even brand-new officers had no difficulty coming up with criteria (critical elements) that they thought necessary for establishing a profession like medicine, law, pharmacology, certified accounting, or education.

When next asked which of these elements are absolutely necessary *to develop law enforcement* into a recognized profession, the responses slowed. This seems to reveal again how officers have never really considered the possibility that law enforcement could become a true profession on that level even though 90 percent of the class raised their hands when asked initially if law enforcement was a profession. This is a strange dichotomy. These issues certainly intersect with the issue of recruiting. If new recruits have never even considered that law enforcement could become a true profession, it seems as if we are starting this ascension process from a very deep hole. On the flip side, if recruiters do not specifically seek those who want a profession or to professionalize, and they never mention to applicants that they are actually looking for those who can develop into true professionals, what hope do we have?

Are We Self-Limiting?

I, on the other hand, have viewed law enforcement as being strikingly close to being a true profession for years now. I did not view law enforcement in this way in the 1960s and early 1970s when I entered the discipline. What this shows, at least for me, is how far law enforcement has come since the early 1960s and how new recruits and recruiters recognize none of this. If a recruit's best view of law enforcement is a blue-collar occupation, we face a real challenge in the coming years. Good recruiting and feeder systems are today becoming critical. We will discuss these in detail later in this chapter.

It Is Time to Wake Up; The Alarm Has Sounded: Most departments do not really consider such professionalization issues as important for the coming decade. "Law enforcement is necessary, so we will be part of the picture no matter what," police administrators often reason. Besides the deficiencies in this reasoning process, we will undoubtedly find that the next decade will be nothing like the last few. Even with the "Defund the Police" movements, many police administrators still ask, why should we even waste our time thinking about the professionalization process?

As for that reasoning process, I would suggest that if a new recruit comes into the job thinking this is all that it can be, and he is then subjected to abusive attitudes and language on the street but later gets an offer for a higher paying job elsewhere, what do you think will happen? There have always been a few rewards in the profession through rank advancement. That has been a narrow doorway, however. Perhaps other professionalization paths within the department should be developed and rewarded. I, on the other hand, think we cannot afford to ***not*** think about the professionalization process if we want ***to protect our officers psychologically****, keep them from* ***becoming tyrants*** *when temptation knocks,* ***remain competent*** in a changing environment, and ***serve our citizens*** as they would want us to serve them.

The Elements of a Profession

Okay, we titled this chapter "Critical Elements for Any Profession," and we have yet to really discuss the first element. So, to get us started, we will discuss several in the paragraphs below that I consider absolutely critical. The rest will be reserved for the next two chapters and for the handy textbox at the end of Chapter 5 as well as for *your thought processes.*

When going through these elements, most will realize that their basic training academy never really presented these issues. That is a shame. Some might say that this subject should, more effectively, be present to the command section. They would, of course, be somewhat correct except that if *everyone* is not indoctrinated into accepting a professionalization mindset and process, it will be difficult for the command section to sell it. The old saying that you can lead a horse to water but you cannot make him drink is appropriate here. We need buy-in at even the entry level.

To begin this examination, we will benefit from seeing where this all started. That makes it easier to understand where we are today and what our goals should be for tomorrow.

The History of Professionalism and Developing Professions

We probably could take this section all the way back to ancient times, especially as it involves highly successful military commanders in the largest empires of the world. We will not do that. We will start from the development of the university system in the Middle Ages. Most of those training schools were originally oriented towards developing people for a religious "profession," a vocation.

Here, the word "profession" was mostly associated with "professing" (a verb) your faith and commitment to God, Jesus, and the church. Later, when other occupations were beginning to be taught in these same universities, this whole idea of committing oneself to higher standards and a career (a lifelong undertaking) took hold in those secular occupations as well. Those employments then began to be viewed as "professions."

It is no surprise that we today share terminology and concepts with those religious orders of old. Concepts like vows, a calling, career, an oath of office, a creed, canons of conduct, a code of ethics, a vocation and so on are still common terms and concepts in most professions today. As we examine these in coming chapters, we will see the religious and faith sentiment embedded in each. These occupations almost seem to become a secular religion, and indeed they are in a sense.

Within certain professions, even today, the oath of office and the vows are still viewed as being very important. Vows made to God but ignored will have consequences, at least as viewed by the religious among us. But before we start to deal with vows, oaths, vocations, and the elements of traditional professions, we will highlight what I think to be a few *critical* elements of any profession, including law enforcement.

Some Critical Elements

As we identify these elements, you may notice what could be identified as differing layers of criticality. The question naturally surfaces: Is a high level of adherence to every one of these elements necessary to have a profession, or can there be a few weaker areas and still have an occupation qualify as a true profession? We will put off that question and all of the nuances of that question off until Chapter 6. Nonetheless, we would want you to think about this layering while we are discussing the three critical elements of a ***calling***, ***recruiting*** and a ***near-fiduciary*** relationship.

A Calling

One of the first critical elements is the concept of a "calling." This seems almost too simplistic and straightforward to need much discussion, but it is a cover-term for a number of additional issues that are quickly apparent after some thought. The calling is the proverbial tip of the iceberg. People in a profession sometimes use this as a distinction between a profession and an ordinary occupation. I think this is not only a valid distinction, it is one of the most important. As to this element, I would like to point out one primary aspect that many do not recognize.

Inherent in a calling is the expectation of a reply. That is somewhat of an illogical thought. The word itself sounds like it entails only a call *going out*, but that is not the whole of it. A look back at what a calling meant in the religious universities reveals much more. In the Middle Ages, callings were all thought of as coming from God and were usually calling someone to the religious life. The important point here is that it came from God! He was calling *you* specifically. It did not originate from you. When God calls, He expects an answer.

Today, with our refuting the very existence of God, many say a calling is something that comes from inside the individual (our inner man). In either case, this is still viewed as originating from somewhere other than *our* (human) temporal consciousness. This inner urge is not something that a person creates (contrives intellectually) in his own mind. Consequently, it must be answered in one of three ways (because we have free-will): the person called must 1) answer in the affirmative, 2) purposely ignore the calling, or 3) answer in the negative, reject it.

Now we can certainly conceive that an intellectual thought process is possible when we want to apply for an ordinary job, but a calling—by the very nature of the word itself—is from outside our intellectual realm. I would argue that those who take a law enforcement job and have not heard this calling (that quiet inner voice that engages our curiosity and desires) should probably look elsewhere for a career as they will not make great police officers, and they will likely not last.

Knowing that the invitation came from beyond us, we are also confronted with the reality that there may be strings attached, so to speak. We do not control what a calling involves since it comes from outside of us. A calling—to take a special, privileged position in society—may involve conditions, responsibilities and obligations associated with it, so we should not accept such a calling lightly, especially if we do not yet really know what is required for that calling. This is particularly true if we believe callings come from God. He will not be pleased if we take a vow and then lightly disregard it over the course of years or even an entire career. Thinking along this line, one can see how accepting this calling really incorporates many of the other elements mentioned in this chapter.

Recruiting the Called

If someone is taking a law enforcement job just until a better paying job comes along, that person really does not bring much to the profession. A calling inherently implies *a career*, with *continuous efforts to improve* as the years go by, a *life-long* endeavor. If God calls you to a livelihood in law enforcement, it is because He thinks you can improve the world during your life, and you can be a good representative of Him.

Nonetheless, because of free will, it is up to us to accept this calling, this challenge, or not. This principle has become increasingly more important ***for recruiters*** today than ***for applicants*** who have just turned 21 years of age and really do not know yet how to pour rainwater out of a boot as far as the profession is concerned [okay, a healthy dose of snark-mania].

Recruiters need to guide applicants and determine *why* someone is applying for the job. On the flip side of this is an assurance that if one is truly called, that person will be able to withstand the adversities, low pay, long hours, and disrespect that are all part of the job, and that person will, in a certain twisted way, enjoy these challenges throughout a long career.

For those who are not sure if they can live up to the demands of working midnight shifts and holidays, dealing with drug abusers and drunks, handling dead bodies, or being civil to those who hate the badge, it is said that ***God does not call the qualified; He qualifies the called***! If one is called, there is a strong probability that this person can do much more than he suspects he can.

Another Example or Two: I would like to relate a story here I think highly relevant. I was recently involved in an effort to resurrect an academy alumni association that had been inactive for a couple of years. I made recruiting pitches to several graduating classes without luck. I knew recruiting would be difficult in this age of cynicism. We had lowered our membership fee to practically nothing and doubled the span of the membership period. Still no luck. We changed the by-laws to make upward mobility much easier within the association. Still no bites. Then I decided to take the opposite strategy with the next class.

When I addressed that class, I said that I was looking for only one or maybe two out of a class that size (150 remaining students). I warned that the coming years would not be easy with the George Floyd death and the coronavirus, but we needed a few people who were willing to represent the profession honorably. Yes, it was the old Marine Corps slogan of, "We are looking for a few good men!" To my surprise, three people stayed after to inquire, and I later found that two had joined. The point here is that any challenging undertaking is not going to appeal to the masses, but there is usually a highly dedicated subgroup in any large group; those who are all-in.

One more short story to bring home my point. When I started at the academy in 1986, our basic training classes were about 60 to 80 people. When I retired at the end of 2017, our basic classes were capped at 170 people, with a long waiting list for each class. The total number of full-time officers in the state had remained virtually unchanged since 1986. This demonstrates how many officers we lose today before retirement. We are in an age in which a calling and a career are not high priorities, which speaks again to the need for good, perhaps even great, recruiting.

The Silver Lining: This all sounds depressing, but I think otherwise. King Solomon said repeatedly that history repeats itself. "The things that hath been, it is that which shall be; and that which is done is that which shall be done: and there is no new thing under the sun," Ecclesiastes 1:9. I believe that as our culture gets darker, as it certainly will, there will likely be a remnant, a cadre, of highly dedicated officers, as there were in the 1960s and 1970s, who will take the profession to the next level, a few champions who are looking for meaning in life, looking to serve something bigger than themselves.

The truth is that because of the way this generation was raised, there might be quite a number of those who want something to fill the hollow existence that our society has sold to so many. Our Generation Z and Millennials may have the strongest "calling" we have seen in years. We just need to be *ready to recruit them* and use them well so that we retain them. This can all stem from good recruiting. It has been my experience that recruiting is more important than even world-class training. [Are you getting tired of that *recruiting* word yet? I am not!]

The Fount: Nevertheless, the bottom line for this mini-discussion is that a calling has *two directions* and recruiting is involved in this. A calling is more than just reporting for duty. I know, I am droning again, but this is so important today. We in law enforcement may be surprised to find that a number of our two current "working" generations (Millennials and Gen Z) may be willing to answer this call **if** we can just identify them. We are, in fact, looking for a few good men and women.

Recruiting Strategies: The element of police recruiting is rarely discussed today. While marshaling a small department many years ago, I eventually developed the philosophy that I would rather ***retain a great employee for three years than a dud for twenty***! This thought process can confuse recruiters. A common idea that taking a less qualified applicant is worthwhile because he will stay at the department simply because he is unable to get a better job ***is a wrong approach***. Besides, even the dud will bail on you the first-time things get really tough. This philosophy of excellence had been verbalized by many over the years before I discovered its importance. Getting the right people is crucial, even if they eventually move on. Heraclitus (an ancient Greek philosopher and commander in the fourth century B.C.) once said:

> **"Out of every one hundred men, ten shouldn't even be there, eighty are just targets, nine are the real fighters, and we are lucky to have them, for they make the battle. Ah, but the one, one is a warrior, and he will bring the others back."**

An All-Important Feeder System: In years past, there were "cadet" programs at *many* departments. There was a vibrant law enforcement "scouting" program. There were internships. There was a very formal, may I say noble, appearance to officers. All of these tended to be strong feeder-programs for recruiting career-oriented applicants, but few exist today. As for suggestions in this area, I think those in the profession today can probably come up with as many good suggestions as I can along this line. The best advice I can give in this area is to not ignore programs or the "things" (whatever those are) that can stir those callings in our next generations.

A Near-Fiduciary Relationship

Our next critical element for all professions but particularly for law enforcement is stressing the need for a near-fiduciary relationship between the profession and the community. One should look at the dictionary definitions for the term fiduciary as a starting point. This is also an overarching element. This concept branches into a number of elements such as the virtues, a code of ethics, canons of conduct, and licensing, all of which are listed in the textbox at the end of Chapter 5. For this chapter, however, we will examine the corporate fiduciary responsibilities.

Unfortunately, we have recently seen allegations of some very serious breaches of conduct at the highest levels of the FBI involving targeting a political candidate and staff in the 2016 elections and thereafter, to include some highly abusive searches. The FBI was previously looked upon as being the shining light in law enforcement, a truly professional organization. These allegations immediately soiled the reputation of that agency and reminded us that serious breaches of honesty can happen within any law enforcement organization. Avoiding those breaches is at the heart of the fiduciary question.

The Difference Between Police and Citizen: I often asked my first-week recruits, what is the difference between a police officer and an ordinary citizen within our state (and within many American states)? I would typically get a number of responses like "policemen carry guns" or "policemen wear uniforms and drive marked cars." After some discussion, I would remind these new officers that virtually anybody who did not have a felony record could, in Indiana, get a handgun license or could simply, after July 1, 2022, strap on a handgun. Likewise, it is not illegal for private citizens to create a uniform that they can wear in public. In fact, they can even wear a badge so long as it does not claim they are a policeman. Private citizens can mark their personal cars with flashy decals and orange revolving lights, and they can actually make a citizen's arrest under certain circumstances in Indiana.

The point for my new students was that there is very little difference between a private citizen and a policeman in Indiana except that policemen are expected to be virtuous and *absolutely honest* when testifying in court or when dealing with the public. Honesty is the lynchpin that all good law enforcement hangs on.

This near-fiduciary relationship with the community is the last highly critical element that we will expose in this chapter. We will finish this chapter by quickly identifying a few bad practices that get officers and departments in trouble with the community. In the next several chapters we will study a few of the spinoffs and consequences of losing this near-fiduciary relationship. But for now, let's discuss a few potentially bad practices.

Some Bad Practices –

We previously mentioned that going to the extremes politically can become a real problem. This involves establishing a number of "zero-tolerance" policies in order to "appear fair" to certain groups. I have always been impressed with how bad zero-tolerance philosophies have been and still are for law enforcement. We, in law enforcement, seem to gravitate towards these. I think this is part of our collective police character. We have regularly initiated this approach for alcohol (drunk driving) and drug abuse and a number of other troublesome areas even to include domestic violence calls.

As a political statement to the public, I suppose this may have some impact and benefit, but it certainly has been a colossal failure in stemming drunk driving incidents or drug addiction or domestic abuse in today's society. This zero-tolerance approach seems to me to be somewhat successful for issues like seatbelt enforcement where there is very little emotional impact on offenders, and the consequences are not so severe. In other areas, these programs have been completely unsuccessful and *very bad* ***for the department*** in many ways.

When I say bad for the department, the thing that really is not considered but is a real detriment is the ***mindset it places in officers***. When I was on the road in my early years, it was not unusual for officers to have a relative "pick up" a somewhat impaired driver or for the officer to actually drive that person home if they were only a few blocks from their home. Officers today can't hardly conceive of such a concept because of the many years of "zero-tolerance" propaganda. I say that this approach is bad for officers and departments because it tends to perpetuate the robo-cop mentality (a very bad thing today) and to reinforce the *us-against-them* mindset which also reinforces the *occupying military force* mindset in both officers and the public which then perpetuates community relations decay.

I will not dwell on this, but there are advantages for ultimately getting help for that impaired driver by having a relative pick up that driver or giving a referral. There are advantages to getting a drug abuser to sign himself into a treatment facility rather than going directly to jail.

A heavy-handed (zero-tolerance) traffic law enforcement policy also has ramifications with the community. This perpetuates the "gotcha" mindset (another really bad approach). A good fiduciary relationship between a department and a community is not rooted on how many arrests the department can make in a year or how many tickets each officer can issue.

Things like being able to talk to a real person when a citizen comes to the police department rather than to a speaker box on the outside of a locked building makes a difference. All of these things create a mindset in the public *and with officers*. When departments encourage officers to participate in community organizations like the Jaycees, the Rotary Club, The Lions, Little League, a car club, or a local church group, this also has an influence on the officer's mindset as well as an influence on the fiduciary relationship between the community and the department.

I will leave it to the reader to research what the word fiduciary should mean in your community and for this purpose. We will see threads of this concept intertwined through the next couple of chapters when we discuss fairness, discretion, and the image a uniform or a marked squad car has on the public.

The three above elements—the concept of a calling, recruiting, and a near-fiduciary relationship—tend to overarch many of the rest and are typically not addressed often in discussions on professionalism or in basic training academies but are pretty important.

In our next chapter, we will summarize the remaining mechanical elements needed for the law enforcement profession and provide a handy checklist of critical elements at the end of the chapter. ❖

Chapter 5

The Critical Elements for the Law Enforcement Profession

A Survey of Attributes

In this chapter, we will examine a number of **specific elements** that seem to be particularly important to the law enforcement profession. We will start with an invitation to a candidate to join the profession, what we previously labeled as "The Calling." If the calling is accepted, this candidate then also affirms all of the ancillary requirements attached to it. For instance, a policeman must be trained, certified and updated annually. In addition, he will likely be working long stretches of midnight shifts in his early career and be assigned the less glamorous details.

Likewise, he is viewed as being a law enforcement officer 24/7. A doctor is a doctor all day, every day. He doesn't just work *as* a doctor *only* during his regular day-hours. A lawyer does not have to punch in to give a legal opinion. If a law enforcement officer sees an armed robbery of a convenience store while off-duty, that officer is expected to act. A street department employee who works for the same mayor and city who sees a chuckhole while off-duty has no obligation to drop off his family on the corner, go to the street department, drive back with a truckload of cold-patch, and repair that chuckhole. His obvious job obligations apply only during the hours he is *actively* working for the city.

A calling to a profession, however, establishes a vocation (there is another very old religious term), a life-long career in which the practitioner is obligated to continuously improve within the areas of that particular discipline. Practitioners typically accept this calling through taking an oath of obligation ("so help me God," a covenant) or making a public vow. This is often at the successful completion of an educational requirement or a testing period. The oath will often incorporate many of the general obligations of the profession, e.g., the code of ethics, etc.

Along this line, the practice of a profession (including law enforcement) requires a high level of virtuous conduct because of the potential of great harm to the community if there is malpractice. Areas like law enforcement, medicine, law, accounting, pharmacology and the like come within such a requirement because of the potential for harm. The harm generated through being a poor trash collector for the street department does not engender a high level of public concern.

The difference here is that the way trash is collected is not particularly technical, and does not require a high degree of sophistication or have a huge immediate negative impact if not done properly. The same can generally be said for the worker who fills chuckholes in the street. Likewise, there is a difference between a bookkeeper and a CPA. A pharmacist is certainly different than the neighborhood drug dealer. We are not yet switching our examination to a discussion of practitioners' virtues—which we will eventually do—but only acknowledging these requirements so that we can see that we need some *mechanical components* within a profession to ensure these standards are met and maintained.

The Foundational Elements

If the discussions in this chapter also appear as if we are, to a degree, looking back to our examination of trades, crafts, etc., we are! The highest elements of those occupations are also interwoven into our examination of this profession. Likewise, starting with a "calling" provides an easy beginning point that most can understand. Consequently, we are now able to flesh-out this study of what we call the professionalization process. So, let us now begin addressing those more complex mechanical elements needed to complete our discussions.

Discretion, again!

Our next element, that we have already mentioned superficially, is the element of discretion. As noted, this is an important one, especially for law enforcement. We find that besides working in an area of critical need, the practitioner typically has, by necessity, a wide range of discretion that must be honorably exercised. Here is where virtue and character come in. A trash collector either picks up the debris left at the curbside or he does not. That is the extent of his discretion. A police officer, on the other hand, must decide if a crime has actually been committed, sometimes in a rather technical area of the law, and whether the person he is investigating actually committed that crime using the admissible evidence available.

Even when there is little question concerning these legal standards in a particular case, the officer still has the discretion as to whether he *should* arrest, or not. How many of us would want an officer to arrest us for every technical traffic law violation we commit while driving to the grocery store? Most motorists would be surprised by how many violations we actually commit in even a short drive. Because of the power given officers, we want them to exercise that large grant of discretion ethically. We want officers to have a substantial amount of self-restraint (discipline) and good judgment (a sense of the greater good) and balance (not be partisan). These all go well beyond the mechanics of making a legal arrest.

Employing Robo-Cops is Not a Good Idea: Perhaps maximizing the number of arrests an officer can make is not the best standard. This begins to get into the area we identified as that near-fiduciary relationship. Is the officer who arrests for *every* technical violation known or uncovered the best officer for our community? Are there other considerations besides straight-line law enforcement that make for a good officer *and* for a better department and community? I think you can see where I am going here.

We will discuss the "sense of the greater good" in detail—what is called a utilitarian worldview, an important concept—in Chapter 11, but here are two questions I would ask you to ponder until we arrive at that analysis. Number one: If an officer arrests for every violation or probable violation he detects, does he then exercise *any* degree of discretion whatsoever? Number two: Does a profession, at that point, lose the designation of being a profession because officers are no longer given any discretionary authority whatsoever? Are they not just arrest-robots then and become only ministerial officers like a clerk rubber-stamping items to be filed? Notice a scary example of this, below.

A Scary Example: If we were to take that maximize-the-arrests approach, we could, in fact, eliminate many officers from the payroll. For every car that enters a roadway, upon exiting that roadway, the driver could be forced to proceed through what today looks like a toll booth, but instead of a toll, the driver would pick up all of the tickets for all of the violations that he committed on his short drive. Speeding, straying over the centerline, following too closely, failure to use a turn signal soon enough before a corner or while lane-changing, and oh so many equipment violations like driver's side window tinted too dark, license plate cover partially obstructing the plate or too dark, muffler too loud, and many more are just a sampling of probable violations.

That two-block drive to the grocery store is not much fun anymore. Nevertheless, this mechanical system of detection and punishment would be absolutely fair and very efficient, but would anyone want to live in that society? With license plate and facial-recognition software available today, such a system is not only possible but economical.

The "Defund the Police" movement initiated in 2020—as ill-conceived as it is—was a social comment by certain communities that, among other things, the police should not be just arrest-machines. Nonetheless, not making any or many arrests—as in the 2020 New York City response to those protests—immediately spiked the incidents of felonious assaults, murders, armed robberies and many other very serious crimes. So, it is pretty obvious that this extreme is not a great alternative either. Perhaps this discretion element really is pretty important for a true profession, and especially for law enforcement.

Canons of Conduct Virtually Unknown in Law Enforcement: Continuing to think more deeply along this line, we will, nevertheless, probably want to give some general guidelines for officers to follow when exercising these huge grants of discretion (which, by the way, will likely get even bigger in the tumultuous years to come). Enter the elements of a really good set of canons of conduct, vision statements, mission proclamations, bureau objectives, directives, and op-plans. These all should include many attributes that professional officers should possess and follow. Here are a few things to consider.

Canons of Conduct

I mentioned at the very start of this book that I believe law enforcement to be very close to becoming a profession. Here, however, is an area in which we need some work.

A Code of Ethics, Then Canons of Conduct: As important as a code of ethics is for giving a general statement concerning the attributes of a profession, most professions also have more specific *canons of conduct* (another term coming largely from religion and the religious universities). What are these? They are typically peer-established standards for guiding practitioners (officers) in particular types of situations. They fill that huge gulf between a general code of ethics and individual department SOPs.

Or perhaps I should say that a set of canons *ought to be there* to fill that gap, but the reality is that very few departments have these.

Canons of conduct, rarely seen in police departments, drill down to specific maxims that should be a part of any profession. They are often viewed as one or two steps above department SOPs or policies. They typically are applied to an entire profession whereas policies and SOPs are applicable only to a specific type of event over which a department or part of a department has jurisdiction.

As an example, the Catholic Church has "canon law" that applies to all Catholic churches and priests regardless of whether the church or priest is located in Germany or Japan or Brazil, or the United States. Because of the structure of law enforcement in America, the requirement that canons of conduct apply to all departments in a jurisdiction must be modified a little. We will make the revelation that since very few states have what look like canons of conduct for their police officers, individual departments need to construct these in America. If these are important for a true profession, and they are, how do we create these? Be patient. We will get there when we arrive at Chapter 7. In the meantime, read about the elements of peer review, certification, and education which all play into a good set of canons.

Peer Review and Standards

Similarly, peer-established standards have long been a recognized element of a true profession as peers are really in the best position to know the requirements of a profession. Have you heard about the medical profession using peer reviewed papers for validating cutting-edge research? Peers are also the ones who have a vested interest in keeping the profession uncorrupted and ethically sound in the eyes of the public (which is largely more of a PR objective than being a real ethical standard, but important nevertheless). Peers are also used to periodically review and update standards, identify needed areas for continuing education, and establish entry, reentry, retention, and decertification standards.

Certification or Licensing and Decertification

Having now mentioned the area of decertification, we should probably also note that all professions have established certification or licensing criteria as an important element in their professions. Licensing is necessary to ensure that an applicant has attained the minimum level of competence for entry into the profession and to ensure there is a mechanical means for expelling someone from the profession when that person does not adhere to those standards, like complying with a continuing education standard.

Education

Having now mentioned education, we must report that nearly all professions have a general educational level for entry to the profession so that applicants have a really good understanding of the culture within which they will be practicing. As mentioned previously, imagine a policeman from Afghanistan or China or North Korea coming to work in America without any indoctrination. One can easily anticipate a number of problems stemming from such a practice.

All professions also require specialized training for entry into that particular discipline. This often requires a certain type of college degree, but in the case of the law enforcement services, this typically requires "academy" training. Along this line, nearly all professions have a minimum continuing education requirement as an important element of the profession. Realizing that things will change, continuing education requirements should be designed to help practitioners adjust to those changes.

A Professional Organization and Journal

Similarly, at least one professional organization is needed to represent the profession to the public and to lawmakers (remember our discussion on the "trades") as well as to keep the profession itself informed of trends. This organization can be and often is used to establish peer standards, conduct peer review, and be a contact-point for the media.

Consider the ABA (American Bar Association) for lawyers or the AMA (American Medical Association) for doctors. A professional organization can also set up a system of discipline for the profession when there is none and especially when total decertification is not required. Likewise, at least one professional journal for a profession is necessary in these modern times to be a conduit for exposing and discussing societal changes and relevant issues, and for keeping the profession's practitioners up to date on new techniques and developments.

Individual Wiggle-Room

Are The Same Standards Necessary Everywhere: Well, there you have it. A few of the elements that all the established professions seem to have and law enforcement probably should have if it already does not. Recognizing that all professions are not the same, however, it is obvious that all professions might not need all of the exact same elements, to the degree another profession does. For instance, medicine may have elements that are not entirely necessary for law enforcement.

Likewise, Indiana has, for example, a rather low minimum general educational level for entry into the law enforcement occupation—a GED—but it has a very strong central academy system to compensate for this. Other states have a less stringent basic training requirement, but then have a substantial annual in-service training requirement. A question often asked is: should all states have the same minimum standards (in effect, federalizing the requirements)? In my opinion, the answer is a resounding NO!

The truth is that water tends to seek its own level. So long as practitioners know what the generally recognized standards are for a profession, virtuous practitioners will strive to make the occupation better through all of the internal means available to them. Over the years I have completed the MP basic training school, the basic training schools in Kansas, Indiana, and Texas as well as a correctional specialist school in the military. All were different, but all produced good and great officers. Since the 1960s, law enforcement has made huge improvements in training (see the textbox at the end of this chapter on past professionalization steps).

So why not federalize these? Even within the same state, substantially different standards can be justified. Indiana has an unusual law enforcement agency that illustrates this point. It is the Indiana Excise Police. This agency and those officers have full law enforcement authority, but those officers spend their time in bars, at frat parties, in after-hours establishments, and even at the Indianapolis 500 Race events. They primarily enforce, among other statutes, Indiana's alcoholic beverage laws. A city officer found sitting in a bar while on-duty would be immediately terminated unless he was specifically assigned that detail for a specific purpose. So, are the exact same standards necessary for all law enforcement officers? Of course not.

The Time is Right: Our occupation waxes and wanes as all things do. I believe we were in a very comfortable time during this last decade, *perhaps too comfortable*! I think we are now ready and capable of taking the next big steps into true professionalism. I think we are already very close, but law enforcement officers in each state ought to ponder the elements of a true profession (again, see the textbox at the end of this chapter) and then see what the deficiencies and weak areas are in their states and departments.

Officers and especially department administrators should then address these internally for their departments. It is often difficult to get legislators and POST (Police Officer Standards and Training) boards to act. Addressing these weak areas individually, in departments, accomplishes ***two very important things***. It quickly starts the process for improvement, and it makes *us* responsible for *us*! When enough of us (department members) start plugging the holes in our leaky ship rather than waiting for outside authorities to tell us what to do, people will notice, including legislators and POST organizations.

How Are We Actually Doing?

Now that we have exposed the many things that law enforcement needs to professionalize, we should ask the question: How are we actually doing? We will look into that in our next chapter, but I think you will be pleasantly surprised to see that we have already accomplished almost all of those things. We truly do not have far to go, if we just will.

Retyping the below textboxes (in Word: Times New Roman, 11) sums up all of this in convenient one-page (printable) listings of these elements and explanations. I think you will find this very handy. One could debate what other elements are needed or that some of the elements listed are not really necessary, but these give a great place to start. It is now *up to you*, officers and administrators, to initiate this process. This will be the step that either pushes us into true professionalism or allows us to fail miserably. It is important to remember: **Leaders, Lead!** ❖

Elements of a Profession

Law Enforcement's Future

1. The practitioner answers ***a calling*** to ***serve*** others or the community through a particular ***discipline***. It is a ***vocation***, a solemn lifetime commitment, a ***career***.

2. The call is answered ***by accepting*** the principles and obligations of the profession through a ***public vow*** or an ***oath*** to God, ***a covenant***. This makes the practitioner a member of the profession (24/7, **a colleague**).

3. The profession serves a ***critical need*** in the community that cannot be satisfied by ordinary citizens stepping forward to accomplish these goals. This critical need is in a ***highly sensitive*** area in which ***unethical behavior*** can have devastating effects.

4. Practitioners must be given and must exercise ***considerable discretion***, particularly in the sensitive areas, in order to accomplish the obligations of the profession.

5. Practitioners must exercise considerable ***self-restraint*** and discipline, because of the serious impact malpractice or indiscretion can have on the community. Because of this sensitive area and the discretion needed, the profession must maintain a ***near-fiduciary***, trust-like, relationship with the community. One of the profession's goals must be to strive for the "***greater good***" of the community.

6. Because of this fiduciary-like relationship, a ***Code of Ethics*** is needed to enumerate the general principles of the profession to the public and to help maintain and guide this **trust** relationship.

7. Specific ***Canons of Conduct*** reflected in a ***Vision*** and ***Mission Statement*** are necessary to implement the Code of Ethics. Periodic ***peer review*** and research must be conducted by those in the

profession to make certain that standards are current and new findings are timely integrated into the profession.

8. Candidates must possess a ***minimum educational level*** to enter the profession that demonstrates a knowledge of the society, history, mores, and the culture they will serve.

9. Because the profession involves a set of complex skills and sophisticated knowledge areas that are beyond those possessed by the general public, candidates must complete ***specialized training*** (**an academy**) for obtaining those complex skills and the sophisticated knowledge for that particular discipline before fully entering the profession.

10. Practitioners must satisfy periodic ***continuing education*** requirements to update knowledge and maintain skills over the course of an entire career. This requirement is often linked to a continuing recertification process or a ***career track***.

11. ***Licensing*** or ***certification*** is necessary to ensure minimum standards are met for virtue and integrity as well as for minimum entrance training and testing standards, and to give a mechanism for decertification for misbehavior or for failure to maintain the continuing education or ethical requirements.

12. There must be at least one ***professional organization*** to represent and discipline members, set standards ***through peers***, and advocate for the profession.

13. There needs to be a ***professional journal*** to update members on new research, peer reviews of and development in the profession, and to act as a forum on these issues.

14. There needs to be a ***peer review*** and a ***disciplinary process*** for alleged violations of the professional standards which can decertify a practitioner for a grievous violation of the standards in order to protect the public welfare and the credibility of the profession.

15. There must be a mandatory element in the recruiting process of the employing agency that verifies that applicants possess the ***higher character virtues*** of honesty, integrity and valor, and an intent to make this employment ***a career undertaking***.

Indiana's Continuing Professionalization Process for career (certified) law enforcement officers

Indiana, like many states, has had a remarkable professionalization process since the 1960s when no training and no state-wide entrance standards were required for police officers. Today, Indiana has one of the few central academies in the nation with over 300 acres of property and dormitory rooms for over 200 officers. The Academy is able to offer not only basic training to three levels of officers but also advanced training in many areas because of an experienced career-oriented staff.

A Continuing Process –

Even with a central academy, oversight, and Constitutional restraints, officers can still become overbearing and even abusive *within* the law. That is why the professionalization process is so important. In these challenging times with resurging pandemics and riots, the professionalization process has become critical. The proper use of discretion and self-discipline are the hallmarks of a true profession. Look how far we have come!

1967 The Law Enforcement Training Board (LETB) was created by statute. Prior to this all departments set their own entrance standards for officers.

1972 Basic training was first required of new officers entering the occupation. Veteran officers were exempt. Newly hired officers had one year to complete basic training, or they would lose their police (arrest) powers until the course was successfully completed. The first mandatory basic training course was held at Indiana Central University (now the University of Indianapolis). All subsequent basic training courses were conducted on the Indiana University's Bloomington campus until the Indiana Law Enforcement Academy (ILEA) building was completed in Plainfield, Indiana.

1975 The main ILEA Academy building was opened in January and classes began that same month.

1993 Continuing education training was first required for regular (career) officers (16 hours annually in any subject covered in the basic course). A 40-hour Pre-basic Course (PBC) was first required as a basic training requirement for police reserve officers. The PBC could also be used to establish a one-year grace period before new regular officers had to complete a full basic training course. Those that did not complete the course in a timely manner lost their police (arrest) powers until successfully completed.

2005 The concept of once certified, always certified was discontinued. The LETB could now revoke an officer's law enforcement certification for misconduct for the first time. An LETB Tribunal was established for this purpose. A Refresher Course was also required for those who had been out of law enforcement for more than two years.

2009 The annual in-service training requirement was increased from 16 to 24 hours. For the first time, two hours of that training were required to be in firearms, two hours were required to be in emergency vehicle operations, and two hours were required to be in defensive (physical) tactics or the use of force.

2015 Reserve officers are, for the first time, required by state statute to have the same amount and kind of in-service training as regular career officers.

2022 A POST system is established within the LETB. **What should our next step be???**

Chapter 6

Implementing the Mechanical Elements

We have now arrived at the tough part of this discussion, implementing all of these "mechanical standards." This chapter is where the rubber meets the road, so to speak. In order to help with this, we will give suggestions and recommendations in hopes of getting officers and departments off to a good start. It is always easier to modify what has already been done than to start from scratch. Every paragraph in this chapter is, nevertheless, a suggestion! Every state is different, and every department is different. That is the beauty of a federal system. We have an entire country that can test good (and bad) responses to challenging times and issues. Recall, if you will, the radical differences between states during the COVID pandemic.

While going through the "Elements of a Profession" checklist at the end of the previous chapter, one will notice, hopefully and thankfully, that we have already satisfied most of those requirements. I am sure that this was a surprise to many officers and administrators. So, this undertaking of completing the process is not so overwhelming after all. In this chapter, we will take a little closer look at those remaining things—the big things—we still need to accomplish. We will discover that even these are not really so big after all.

You may notice by the end of this book that there are a few other areas, that I label as "weak" areas (the little things), that we should probably address as well, but none of those are absolutely necessary for creating a true profession and honest men can disagree on those points. Those areas are, of course, up to you to ponder, discuss, and solve in your individual departments.

A Few of Our Biggest Remaining Challenges

The 2020 riots and burnings, in theory, stemmed from an improper police interaction with the community—the George Floyd incident—but we quickly found that the real continuing power behind those riots was from a much more sinister element than originally thought. The push towards one-world governance through *any means possible* has many high-level supporters in nearly every nation of the world. The *any means possible* element involves many illegal and immoral avenues which often result in direct confrontations for law enforcement. This results in some challenging situations. Nevertheless, the subject of police professionalism was in *bad need of re-examination* even before 2020.

Although not quite as scary as a hidden and potentially lethal virus, a dormant professionalization process can, in the long run, be even more destructive to our society and police departments. With all of the things that are now surfacing in the news about the FBI's role in the 2016 elections, the 2020 elections, home searches, and other events—shameful events—perhaps we will soon be saying that this subject is, in fact, even more frightening than a virus outbreak.

Most of the "elements" listed in the text boxes at the end of Chapter 5 are pretty straightforward and easy to understand although that does not mean they will be easy to implement or attain. Our officers and administrators are smart people and will be able to begin the implementation process as soon as they *begin to recognize* and ***accept*** these as crucial. There is the difficult aspect of this.

Three Problem Areas

As always, we want to identify problem areas—as well as the easy to-dos—so we do not spend a lot of time on gee-whiz issues. There are elements that have been strongly proposed over the years as necessary for upgrading the police occupation. In order to get us moving, I will open three of these alleged deficient areas for discussion. You will see that I do not necessarily agree with those areas being a problem, but you must ultimately be the judge. These include: **1)** a mandatory **college degree** for all officers, **2)** advanced **writing skills**, and **3)** more "**social justice**" training.

As for this last one, I contend that if this were to center on *honest* historical perspectives of our profession, our country, and the Founding Fathers, I might agree. Nearly everything that has been said here, however, is a distortion or a bold-faced lie [sorry, can't mince words]. I see none of the social justice agenda as beneficial for the police profession.

The College Education Question

We have previously said that specialized training is a requirement of nearly all professions and is important for the law enforcement profession as well. We next asked if this meant that all should have a college degree as many professions now require. I am going to make arguments for and against certain elements being more important to the professionalization process than others. The concept that some elements are more important than others will probably not be challenged by many, but the specific elements that I identify may be, and this is probably one of those. Again, this will be one of the areas that I beat up pretty severely.

Debated Since the 1960s: Making a college degree mandatory for law enforcement has been hotly debated since the 1960s when The National Advisory Commission on Criminal Justice Standards and Goals looked at this potential requirement. Indiana, in fact, has *one* *of the least stringent* general education requirements of any state—a G.E.D.—for entry into the occupation. As mentioned earlier, Indiana makes up for this, I think, by a really good central academy system. We will not examine what this involves here, but those Indiana officers who have had experience with other states can attest to this.

One Indiana law enforcement department that prefers a two-year associate degree is the Department of Natural Resources. Their Conservation Officers are fully empowered to enforce all criminal statutes within the state and are highly regarded. This department is relatively small, however, and has had a really good unofficial feeder system through one of the community colleges in which potential applicants can obtain an associate degree in areas related to natural resources or law enforcement or both. This particular feeder system satisfies most of what was mentioned earlier about the benefits of good recruiting. This feeder system has worked really well for this department for many decades!

A much larger department, the Indiana State Police, attempted to implement a college degree requirement several years ago but found after a very short time that they could not recruit enough applicants to keep up with retirements. That college degree requirement was subsequently abandoned.

A former state police superintendent told me that they also experienced problems during that time by hiring applicants straight out of college who had no life experiences and were put into a position of great authority. Of course, one of the strongest arguments in favor of requiring a degree is that these candidates have the drive and focus to succeed. I agree. However, they are not an exclusive subset of society, meaning they are not the only people who have determination and focus.

Giving absolute preference to these types (degree holders) has many "social justice" ramifications as well that we will not pursue here. Unlike becoming a medical doctor, police officers truly need the training and experience of dealing with real people in real-world stressful situations (social skills). Young people get these from a stress-academy and from living and working in society before being hired in a police position.

Comparing Other Professions –

By contrast, medical doctors need a high degree of knowledge in the disciplines of biology, anatomy, chemistry, physiology and the like that are available primarily in the university environment. Consequently, college is critical for doctors but not absolutely essential for police officers, I believe. The only high-level didactic knowledge needed by entry-level police officers is a really good grasp of law and procedure, and some advanced writing skills.

A second very important limitation *today* in requiring all police applicants to have a college degree is that a college education, i.e., indoctrination, is to a certain degree antithetical to law enforcement employment. Law enforcement is still a para-military hands-on occupation. The extreme views within the secular humanism and similar worldviews (examined in detail in Chapter 11) do not align students with being able to subordinate themselves to authority, exercise a high degree of humility, or recognize divine morality.

It is well documented that students entering college today are indoctrinated into a worldview that their parents often do not recognize when they return home. These students were actually more in line with what it takes to become a good police officer upon graduation from high school than they are upon graduation from certain colleges, although even some high school curricula have now changed to being very woke.

We have previously mentioned reinstituting "cadet programs" in departments as a possible feeder system. This seems more beneficial for creating really good officers than relying on today's "college environment." **A hugely surprising fact that many do not realize is that the George Floyd incident occurred in Minnesota, *one of the few states that actually requires a college degree*!** Interesting! Those college degrees obviously do not inoculate officers from bad practices. We could say much more on this, but we won't.

The really important didactic skills needed by police officers—the law and writing skills—can all be presented very successfully in an academy setting. The really tricky part of this is getting these, especially the writing skills, reinforced in the departments' in-service training program. This has been pretty much a total, miserable failure in the past. Very few departments incorporate writing skills within an annual in-service training curriculum. But before getting into this, let us look first at this law requirement.

If I claim that a college degree is not absolutely needed to be a great police officer, that would infer that I believe there must be a rather challenging "law" requirement in the academy. The answer to this is, absolutely YES! You will see just how challenging I think this should be by the end of this chapter.

Law Classes: The academy law classes should be one of the gatekeepers to the profession (even beyond the selection process). Unfortunately, many academy law classes are very watered down, VERY watered down. This is partly because departments and academies do not want officers washed out because of a failed law exam after an expensive and time-consuming selection process. [Here is a logical challenge: how can you keep from having someone washed out if he is highly watered down? Sorry, don't even waste your time thinking about this.]

I have witnessed officers doing things that would make them cringe if they had a truly deep legal knowledge in those areas. During my long career and several relocations, I have graduated from a number of police basic training academies and one correctional specialist school, and I can personally testify that the only in-depth and comprehensive academy law classes that I have had were the Indiana basic academy law course and an FBI National Academy law course. The rest were pretty pathetic!

Recommendation: An academy law course needs to encompass what is generally known (in universities and law schools) as Constitutional law, criminal law and criminal procedure, and these need to be taught in a 300-level caselaw format. Why a caselaw format? The caselaw format relates the principles of the law to *real-world* scenarios. The practice of an instructor just quoting a statutory enactment (a law) or a constitutional clause is practically worthless in conveying the deep meanings of those provisions.

This deep knowledge is actually more important for police officers than it is for first-year law school students, deputy prosecutors, or *even* U.S. Supreme Court justices! That is quite a statement. However, law students, prosecutors, and judges can take several hours to research every jot and tittle of a law. A street officer needs a comprehensive, deep-working knowledge of the law that he can recall at a moment's notice when involved in a fray, a domestic dispute, or a use of force incident, to name just a few. Most do not have that depth of knowledge and just wing-it. Winging it is not a good idea in today's environment.

This training approach is rarely even attempted in academies today. A police academy graduate should actually be able to pass the criminal law and criminal procedure portions of a state bar exam. In addition to this, an officer must be well versed in several other areas of the law, e.g., traffic law, juvenile law, juvenile procedure, and several civil procedures. A handy listing of these subjects is placed at the end of this chapter. Those additional law areas are pretty self-explanatory and do not need further explanation here.

Writing Skills and Communicating

Here is a controversial area! A second area of academic excellence that *should be forced* upon officers, I think, are the advanced writing skills. Some Millennial and Gen Z officers today are having a few problems with their somewhat limited face-to-face verbal skills due to the social media phenomenon. Older officers have typically been much stronger in this face-to-face area. Those officers—coming from that more traditional mold—are, in fact, what I call great Benevolent Speakers [kind, compassionate, non-aggressive discoursers, meaning great BSers, a technical designation totally understood by all veteran officers].

They are great at calming domestic conflicts by being able to empathize with both sides or refereeing irate motorists at traffic accident scenes by being helpful to both drivers. They can talk a suicidal client off a bridge who thinks there is no hope and reassure a distraught mother who has a missing child.

Almost **all** officers, however, are weak, some pathetically weak, in the writing skills. When I started in law enforcement, many departments had handwritten reports. *Thank goodness* we no longer have to read longhand reports! Typewriters and then computers have helped immensely in this area, and grammar and spelling checkers have made a world of difference as well. Nevertheless, officers still struggle mightily with narrative and content which are, beyond any shadow of a doubt, the most important aspects of any police report.

Police officers tend to be action oriented. That is what attracts many of them to the police services. They hate sitting behind a keyboard and always have. That is why I mentioned, several paragraphs above, that they should be **forced** to take advanced writing classes. Even though a good criminal law course can be very challenging, most officers view this as part of being a *law enforcement* officer. For that class, they will bite the bullet.

Police report writing is a little different. It is viewed as a necessary evil. And unfortunately, most college writing classes miss the mark. The closest thing that academia has to what is needed in law enforcement is called "expository writing" but even that falls short. College courses accomplish the "exposing" element pretty well but do not really know *what to expose*, which often involves very technical areas within law enforcement. Being a generalist (i.e., he is just a "bad guy") does not work in the court system.

Ask an experienced college writing professor what the necessary legal elements are for an armed robbery case report, how to write a search warrant application for a dwelling, how to justify impounding a vehicle, or how to write a civil commitment affidavit, and you will generally be able to reduce these Ph.Ds. down to babbling idiots. Police report writing is just too technically specific to benefit much from general expository writing principles.

As tough as designing an extensive academy writing course is, that is what is needed in every basic training course. In such a class, content is king! Incidentally, an academy *final writing exam* at the very end of the academy is also a great way to gauge if officers *really* understand the legal and other technical requirements of the job. This is rarely done. In fact, many academies do not even have a real final exam for the writing segment of the basic training course.

Scenario Based Exams: Such writing exams should include all that the new officer has learned (sorry, should have learned) in his writing, law, tactical, and procedures classes. These would include how to subdivide and organize a report, how to establish a rock-solid probable cause for *each* charge, how to write his stopping justification, why he drew his weapon or any other use of force, and how to justify the search (of the car, house, or person) just to mention a few critical areas, ***just like he will be required to produce* at the department**. What a concept! [Oops, snarky again.]

Writing a simulated investigative report (even more difficult) as part of the final course exam would also show if the officer can identify the elements of a potential charge after completing an investigation, comply with protocols for scene processing, document proper evidence collection, protect the chain of custody, conduct interrogations, and so much more, in a way that mirrors what he will really be required to do on the job. I ask my officers reading this, is that what you were tested on at the end of your basic training academy? I pretty much know the answer to that.

Well, if you think officers dislike *academy* writing classes, most of which do not reflect the above criteria, just ask them about the need for in-service advanced writing classes. That is why ongoing in-service writing classes are ***virtually nonexistent*** in this country. Yes, I mean the

entire country! Should we force these types of classes on officers? You can easily see my thoughts on this, but you be the judge.

No Excuses, but Still No Acceptance –

One final point on this [yes, I am beating this subject to death as well]. Many years ago, I designed a prefabricated (i.e., *very* easy to use) in-service writing course. I announced and showed this to every basic training class coming through the academy and told them that I would supply this for free to any department wishing to incorporate it into their annual in-service training. In all of those years, I received ***only one*** call about this class (there are over 500 departments in Indiana) and that department never followed up after the initial call. This, again, gives a pretty clear look at the police mindset on this subject.

In this prefabricated writing course, a facilitator would need no writing background whatsoever and only an hour or so of familiarization exposure to be able to present it successfully. It was as user-friendly and easy as I could design it. I offered this course to all of my promotion school students after I retired and am still waiting *for that first question* about this course. I have loved policemen and what they do since a very early age, but I also recognize some huge shortcomings within our profession. This is one of them.

More Than Just Writing Skills: Largely unnoticed by administrators are the many ancillary benefits of improving reports *after* the academy that have nothing to do with writing *per se*. An officer's on-the-street conduct, especially with borderline officers, will improve with better reports. When supervisors actually *require* officers to submit comprehensive reports, what is really being demanded of these officers is that they "tell on themselves." Who wants to say how poorly he handled a call? Likewise, if an officer is lazy, he must either omit reporting on that part of the incident, or he must lie. Conversely, a great officer can report what a good job he did on a call even when a supervisor was not around.

Demanding complete, logical, well-organized, reader-friendly, psychologically-compelling reports require that officers address all elements of a crime, not just the most obvious; it demands they write a report that uses some psychological techniques that tend to convince the reader of the rightness of the officer's claim; and it demands that they tell on themselves, how did they do on this call? These and several other benefits stem from improved reports that go well beyond just placing barely adequate words on a piece of paper [sorry, I mean in a computer data bank; remember, you are listening to a guy who still uses a chalkboard].

Recommendation: All basic training academies should institute *an aggressive* writing course. An advanced writing course should also be incorporated into in-service training so that it becomes evident to officers that producing really good police reports is vitally important to their administrators.

The person who replaced me as the writing instructor at the academy when I retired did something really brilliant. I wish I had thought of this. He went to the Indiana Prosecuting Attorney's Council, and over the course of a couple of years, found that those deputy prosecutors ***had no problem whatsoever*** in coming up with quite a number of areas for improvement in police writing skills. What a surprise! He then began addressing those "very specific" areas in his course. I would make the suggestion that local police administrators could employ this same tactic on a yearly basis with their deputy prosecutors or county attorneys. We might be surprised at what we find.

Social Justice, Worldviews and Our Historical Foundations

A third important but nebulous area that has surfaced in recent years for "professionalizing" the occupation is unfortunately remedial. Like the first two, this one is not addressed in most academies because most "critical" subjects for a basic training curriculum were determined in the 1960s when the federal government mostly forced states to start basic training programs. Since then, much has changed. Basic training students now come to the academy with very little, if any, background in government, civics, and U.S. Constitutional principles, or in world and U.S. history.

This is a complex issue. I believe that most basic training curricula across the country badly needs updating. However, much of this, suggested by the Left, like equity and CRT training, is absolutely the wrong approach. In years past, things like softening the appearance of the police uniforms were suggested. Most of those 1970 suggestions have proved to be less beneficial than originally thought. Not recognizing the huge gaps, however, that now exist in the general education reservoirs of new officers in areas like civics, government, and Constitutional provisions *is negligence.*

These deficiencies allow the bait of "social justice" claims to hook young officers. If these subjects were properly addressed somewhere, at the academy or in the public schools, the claims of the *1619 Project* would no longer have any weight. These were areas stressed in secondary education in the 1960s and thought to be *totally unnecessary,* back then, for a police academy curriculum.

Recommendations–Picking Up the Slack: Today, we see young people who do not realize what terrible things happened in Russia, China, Cambodia, and Venezuela when socialism took over. Today, young people are not as patriotic as they once were. Today, young people do not hear about how brave our Founding Fathers had to be in order to bring our republic into existence.

Should it be the responsibility of an academy to make up this ground when high schools and colleges do not teach on these important subjects? Of course not, *BUT* the reality is that **we must now shoulder** this ancillary *but very important* duty if we are to produce really good officers. Unfortunately, the extent to which these missing educational components impede an officer's dedication, patriotism, career view, and basic knowledge of U.S. Constitutional provisions is profound and largely unrecognized.

Recommendation – Scenario Training: Secondly, basic training academies need to increase scenario training in most states. Indiana just increased its basic training course one full week to accommodate increased scenario training situations. Why? Because so many new officers have not been out in the real world long enough to have that all-important practical experience. Entire books have been written on our Millennials and Gen Z generations who often live in their parents' basement years after graduating high school. Many have never held a job for more than a year. Some move directly from a college environment to the police ranks. Previously, police recruits brought military experiences or four to five years of prior employment experience with them. They tended to be married much earlier and supported a family and made regular mortgage payments *before* entering the police services.

Today, more than ever, this increased scenario training is probably necessary to show new officers how to respond specifically to many more situations than was needed in prior years. On the other end of the spectrum, more advanced didactic training is also needed in areas that will make officers aware and appreciative of the things done for their benefit by the Founding Fathers and other patriotic heroes. This is needed to make them bond with the American dream and appreciative of American exceptionalism.

One could also argue that this lack of real-world experience can lead to officers resorting to their firearms too quickly because they feel so threatened. In years past, people in that age group typically had one or two fights in the school parking lot before they graduated [myself included]. They experienced corporal punishment in the schools. They were not coddled by parents or special interest groups. In short, they were better prepared for the hard knocks of life.

Collegiality –

Collegiality is a sense, a feeling, that sometimes happens within a profession or organization. This can be perpetuated by certain structural elements within a department. We mentioned that we need to get new officers to bond with the American ideal. Well, bonding with fellow officers is also a powerful tool. This is more than just having a working relationship. This forms ***an informal but strong covenant*** between and among officers.

This has so many benefits that we could write an entire chapter on this alone. This is an area that is largely up to department administrators to infuse into a department. Instilling a sense of collegiality between officers supports officers in tough times. It pushes officers to be better. It unifies a department. To a certain degree, it also helps instill a sense of oneness with the community. Even something as simple as a department picnic in the summer or a Christmas party in the winter can help.

Covenant vs. Contract: Having now mentioned the term covenant, I have one last subject for this chapter concerning this concept. This has to do with worldviews. Collegiality, perspectives, historical awareness, and virtues all come within what I will call the overarching topic of worldviews. Worldviews can and often do incorporate all of these elements. We will devote an entire chapter, Chapter 11, to worldviews. The concept of covenant also comes within this overview.

A sense of a covenant relationship is not realistically explored today at any level. A critical principle here is that a covenant can be one-sided and internal, and is significantly different than a civil "contract."

In the book of Genesis, God demonstrated this concept for our benefit. He made a one-sided covenant with Abram. Abram took several sacrificial animals and divided them up as was usual when making a two-sided agreement, but God then put Abram into a deep sleep and God completed the covenant process alone, signifying that God would do what he said even if Abram and every one of his descendants were unfaithful. This was a model, I think, for a true profession.

This was a one-sided covenant in which a beneficiary could commit all forms of wrong but the grantor would still adhere to his obligations. With such a covenant, an officer would honor his agreement even when assaulted and slandered by the public. An officer would keep his word even when someone threatens to sue him. He would do what was best for the citizens even when they seemed to turn on him, e.g., Defund the Police. Whenever a party breaches the agreement in a civil contract, there is no obligation for the other side to complete his obligations. The contract is "broken."

Perhaps this is the way that accepting a calling—yes, back to that again—should be viewed, even today. A candidate to the profession agrees to conduct himself nobly and virtuously regardless of outside influences or corruptions. Officers perform their duties and obligations because of what they said they would do, not because of what outsiders think of, do to, or for them. This arrangement is not a *good response* for a *good response*. It is: I will be true, no matter what.

Viewing their employment in this way eliminates expectations that the public should love them and appreciate all they do. Now, in some communities, this is largely true, but even in those communities, officers will often be disappointed with certain community responses. Establishing a covenant relationship, in an officer's mind, makes officers *look inward* for reasons to perform admirably, a very important perspective. It tends to make an officer noble. He will know this when he does it.

This also provides a foundation upon which an officer can improve over an entire career. Attempting to develop this thought process with new officers is rarely tried. It develops a worldview that makes good officers great. I know I strayed a little into the virtues here, but it was a logical place to address this [sorry, it won't happen again, at least until Chapter 7, but when we arrive there, you'd better tighten your seatbelt].

A True Oddity: I recently attended the funeral of a former Indiana state police officer who was older than I was by more than fifteen years. I will not bore you with how we became great friends, but our paths crossed in so many distant lands and ways that it seemed providential. He was a GREAT mentor. He had been retired from the state police for about thirty years. At his funeral, two separate supervisors who had also been retired for decades brought two separate letters to read at the service. These had come from people who had been given a ticket by Dean.

They had sent in these letters to his supervisors exclaiming how professional he was. Both supervisors said that they had never had this happen except for that one letter (one to each supervisor) during their entire careers. We sometimes hear urban legends on this type of thing, but the reality is that practically no policeman knows another officer who has had such a letter sent to a department supervisor.

My mention of this is simply to relate that as rare as this is, and *it is **rare***, it can happen, and it is within the grasp of a few officers on nearly every department, if they will think along this line.

Viewing the Big Picture

Summing up these elusive issues, we must recognize that training a torrent of new officers to replace officers who did not make it to their 20-year mark is hugely expensive. Taking a criminal procedure class without a really good foundation in U.S. Constitution provisions limits the results. Dealing with the public without a saint's perspective will usually lead to cynicism and bitterness.

A police officer's main duty, in the broadest sense, is to maintain the *status quo*. If officers do not know or care about the United States, why should we expect them to help maintain the *status quo*? It is discouraging that we must even discuss these issues in a basic training curriculum, but times have changed. These are all remedial subjects, but unfortunately, the woke cohort is upon us, and those new officers have no background in these areas whatsoever to gird them.

Recommendations: Basic training academies should have at least five hours of "Introduction to Criminal Justice Systems" which should include a discussion of law enforcement and American history that incorporates the principles important to the Founding Fathers. We need to train who the American heroes were and what heroic acts they performed and how they sacrificed. This discussion should include a substantial segment on the writing of the Declaration of Independence and the Constitution, and it should include a substantial discussion on the mechanical elements of a profession (beyond occupational ethics, which should still be given in a separate academy class).

This indoctrination should also include an exposure and discussion on worldviews—i.e., the attributes expounded in the utilitarian worldview, in the Judeo-Christian worldview, and in other views—as well as the most desirable virtues for police officers (discussed later in this book under the "template of chivalry"). In addition, two to three hours should be specifically devoted to Constitutional provisions *before* the criminal law course even begins. In-service training should pick up on these themes whenever possible.

Some Thoughts on Staying Nimble

When I attended my first civilian police academy, basic riot formations were taught with 36-inch batons because every officer was expected to perform those duties in the chaotic environment of those days. Not that many years earlier, in my basic MP school, riot formations were also taught using riot shotguns with 18-inch attached bayonets. My, how things changed in that short period of time.

Likewise, direct head strikes and throat jabs with the MP baton were just being phased out of the training curriculum at that time. My MP training manual, which I still have, clearly shows all of these techniques. I kept this as *I knew* that officers in the future would have a hard time believing that these techniques were ever taught. Likewise, Supreme Court decisions were coming down at what seemed like a weekly basis. Yes, things were very dynamic in the training arenas in those days. We need to accept a similar mindset today.

What was accomplished in the 1960s and 1970s was admirable, even spectacular, with the establishment of basic training academies, entrance standards, the programs coming out of the Law Enforcement Assistance Administration, as well as the standards established through Supreme Court decisions. We find ourselves again in a like situation. Perhaps it is time to re-evaluate our goals and prepare for the coming decades.

I mentioned at the very start of this book, and several times since, that I think law enforcement is very close to being able to become a true profession. Nevertheless, these last few hurdles are significant, not because they are so tough but because we in law enforcement are *status quo* people. We in law enforcement ignore developing situations and history and community needs, and we ***fight change***, tooth and nail. Perhaps our willingness to do these few remaining things will be a good gauge on whether we ultimately deserve to be called professionals, or not! ❖

A Checklist–Summing This All Up –

There are, of course, other classes that could arguably be added to a modern basic academy training curriculum to compensate for the differences between what police candidates need today compared to what they needed in 1967. In the last chapter, we provided a checklist on the elements of a profession. We will now also provide, below, a quick-reference guide on some of the items yet to be accomplished—mostly training shortfalls—in our professionalization process. I believe we are so very close to becoming a true profession, even if unrecognized by practitioners, that this goal is only steps away. But clearing these hurdles with our present mindset is yet another question. The time is now right. Strike while the iron is hot!

So, here are a few areas that still need some work:

Items Yet to Accomplish
The Police Professionalization Checklist

- An aggressive basic training law course including: Constitutional law, criminal law and criminal procedure (using the caselaw method); First Amendment and Second Amendment rights and limitations on officers (probably offered for the first time in many states); juvenile law and procedure; traffic law and procedure; civil liability law and some civil law having to do with civil commitments; civil process for civil decree enforcement including the subjects of internment camps; criminal emergency decree enforcement procedures including incarceration procedures; the writ of habeas corpus; and martial law.

- An aggressive writing program – with writing *and policing* skills incorporated into a final basic training course writing exam (stressing content).

- Covenants and Professional Responsibility Obligations.

- Introduction of Criminal Justice Systems material into the basic training curriculum including a discussion on law enforcement and American history.

- Material and discussions on Constitutional provisions important for law enforcement and the Declaration of Independence.

- Our Founding Fathers' Worldviews, stories, and quotes.

- World Ethics, i.e., Worldviews [beyond "religious ethics"].

- The mechanical aspects of a true profession (presented in basic training) so that new officers are prepared for professional development classes at the department.

- Fulfillment of deficient or weak elements in the "Element of a Profession" checklist.

- The Important Virtues for Professional Law Enforcement.

- Establishing (at least within the department) some canons of conduct and related policies and documents.

It will be difficult to find current academy instructors who want to present these subjects since these are not traditional police subjects, and there are few within an academy staff who are prepared to instruct in these subjects. We, nonetheless, badly need to develop in these areas. ❖

Chapter 7

Virtue, Character, Nobility, and Other Really Abstract Ideas

If you think that the previous chapters have taken us to places that most law enforcement practitioners have never contemplated, it is time to fasten your seatbelt—again! This will be a mega-chapter. Most readers will have to take a break after this chapter to really process what has been said because of the breadth of the material covered. We are now ready to consider in some detail which of the many virtues a practitioner must possess and practice to be considered a true law enforcement professional.

We will be investigating concepts in this chapter and subsequent chapters like what the terms virtue, valor, gallantry, and justice mean *in a practical sense*. We are about to ask, is there a practical difference between ethics and morals? What is truth? Does faith influence how well law enforcement practitioners perform? What should officers do if they consider a decree unquestionably immoral, illegal, or unconstitutional? Is it likely that officers will be asked to enforce extreme decrees in the future? How about martial law? Will the writ of habeas corpus be suspended in the career-span of these present officers?

These are but a few of the head-scratchers that our current generation of officers may (probably will) be facing. How should they react? From this point on, we will be examining those subjects that we identified at the beginning of this book as unquestionably the most difficult in this professionalization process. We announced at that time that we would start with the easy concepts but then warned that we would eventually arrive at the truly complex ones. Well, we have now arrived! Sorry.

These ideals of morals, virtue and character are actually part of the bedrock we identified in the first two chapters which are necessary for a true profession and real professionals. As mentioned there, we delayed discussing these—even though our "building" progression seemed somewhat out of order—until we had poured a few solid foundations. This and subsequent chapters will not only look at these bedrock issues but will also give a number of likely scenarios where these will come into play in the near future and some practical ways to prepare for those situations. In order to help with this examination, as in prior chapters, the first thing we must do is lay the groundwork and define the terms.

Defining Terms: When dealing with the concepts in this chapter, defining the terms is a major undertaking as so many of these terms are ambiguous. Are ethics and morals the same thing? How should we define chivalry? What is truth? Perhaps we should start with this last question as this is so basic, and it has deviated substantially from what it meant just a few generations ago. This is not to say that this has not been a contentious concept for millennia. Pontius Pilate famously exclaimed at Jesus' trial, "What is truth?"

Confusion in the Ranks: We have already hinted at some of these definitions. Now, we will get specific and show how they apply in the real world. Today, graduates of nearly every American university have been indoctrinated into believing that truth is whatever it is for that person. According to academics there is no absolute truth. Right and wrong do not really exist. Ethics and morals are what you believe they are. This can be very unsettling for new police officers who must enforce *traditional* standards.

I believe this is one of the reasons we have such a high turnover rate in the occupation today. If officers cannot, in their own minds, believe they are doing honorable things to keep society afloat, every arrest can chip away at an officer's image of himself. Is he mean-spirited for arresting this person? Is he uncaring? After all, every arrest impacts the arrestee's ability to support his family and get a good job. Every arrest digs deeply into an arrestee's wallet or someone's savings account, and every arrest shapes the arrestee's image of himself. Officers need to know that what they are doing is noble!

The obvious problem here (obvious to those of us who are a little older) is that if Jerry thinks abortion is immoral but Jenny thinks it is a woman's choice, who is right when legislators (representing voters) and courts (representing Constitutional principles) deal with this subject? If Gus thinks that self-injecting a strong narcotic into his body is morally reprehensible, but Billy thinks it is his body and whatever he wants to do with his body is his business, who is right? And then, of course, the final important question with all of this is, if a thousand people have widely divergent opinions on these issues, who is correct, and *what is truth*? Laws within a society crumble when large portions of that society cannot agree on the benefits of a law. This reveals the fact that social norms are even more basic (and important) than the laws themselves.

What is Truth?

With such a worldview (secular humanism and others, see Chapter 11), the word truth cannot convey an absolute standard when *everybody* defines it differently, and therefore, the concept violates itself (its dictionary meaning). It cannot be what it claims to be: truth!

Some say that this dichotomy only occurs in the social justice areas. The areas of the hard sciences still have and will always have "truths." Two plus two equal four. Period! Beliefs cannot influence the hard sciences. Really?

This is the way I used to think until recently when I saw nearly the entire world affirm that there are way more than two sexual or gender orientations. In some states, boys can now enter girls' restrooms if they feel like they are a girl today. High school boys can now compete in girls' track competitions. Unemancipated juveniles can decide to have sex-change surgeries (mutilations) performed—even over a parent's objections—if, during this confusing time of life, they feel uncomfortable within the sexual body into which they were born. Who didn't feel uncomfortable during that time of life? The really amazing thing is that nearly the entire world has bought into this. This has to be motived by something other than reason, perhaps some unseen dark forces.

A "belief system" (a worldview) has overtaken the sciences and logical processes in oh so many areas today. It used to be said that it does not matter what you think; what you think does not change the "truth." That may now only be correct at the "Judgment Seat." Whether a young person has a certain combination of X or Y chromosomes is as much of a hard science as two plus two, but try to live with that reality today, and you will bring angry mobs down on you and your family.

Truth is: Having mentioned "The Judgment" as a "truth" *outside* of man's control leads us into a true (or more accurately, *the* true) solution for this problem and for our considerations. The simple *practical* solution is to have one person set the standard for truth who is all-knowing. Then we *have* truth! That one person is, as we have previously said, God (unless you, like so many today, do not believe in Him, either). As for street officers, having a religious belief system is certainly helpful in performing the day-to-day duties of the job. Even without a religious foundation, however, officers who acknowledge a supreme being or an "intelligent designer" can have a sense of the truth. Moral teachings are then clear. Societal standards are justified. Long-standing statutes are reasonable. Truth is truth, and—more importantly for our discussion—**an officer's duties *are noble*!** ***Blessed*** are the peace keepers.

For all of our ethical discussions, we will assume there is a God as this is the only logical foundation, I believe, on which to base such an expansive examination. Having set this as our maxim, we can now look at a few definitions. Let's start with a tough one while we are still somewhat fresh.

Truth, Morals, and Ethics: The Core

More Definitional Confusion: As mentioned earlier, I recently heard my pastor define **ethics** in a way that seemed to me to be up-side down. He used ethics as the basis for the traditional church beliefs and **morals** as the standard for a particular society. I had always envisioned morals as the unchanging higher (divine) law and ethics as the worldly adaptations of those principles. I had often heard of "professional ethics" which seemed to support my perspective on this. I went home and consulted several dictionaries. To my dismay, I discovered many instances of what I called "circular definitions" in this area.

I would invite you to take a trip into this spiraling *Alice in Wonderland* investigation as well, but have some aspirin nearby as you will then find that these two terms, morals and ethics, are just a few of many ethical terms that have such circular definitions. What do I mean here by circular definitions? The dictionary definition of morals, in each dictionary, uses the word ethics to define it, and the definition of ethics uses the word morals to define it, a migraine in the making. Rather than leaving my readers to scratch their heads in bewilderment, I have decided to define these and other terms for *our* purposes so that we can have some common ground.

Unchanging Morals, Changing Ethics: One definition of ethics (in the Merriam-Webster dictionary) mentioned earlier is: ***the science** of morals as it endeavors to divide men into the good and bad*. We touched upon this in Chapter 2. Morals, for our purposes, is God's law; ethics is man's. This leads us quickly into the practical area of determining what "virtues" mean in real life.

The Virtues: I will define **virtue,** for our purposes (another really ambiguous term), as a general concept incorporating *honesty*, *morality*, and *integrity* into its meaning (Merriam-Webster and Microsoft Thesaurus). In previous times, virtue also meant manly strength and inherent power. Most have a sense of what honesty means. Morality signifies the highest (Godly) law, and integrity is our ability to maintain morality over long periods of time. Why is this important?

Virtues, as we will be using the concept, are part of our Judeo-Christian ethic that stems from the bedrock morals. We will see in Chapter 11 that not all worldviews stem from bedrock morals. You will easily recognize this when we start to discuss some of the occultic worldviews. Consequently, not all attributes are virtues. Some world-view attributes are very evil. I will give a one-sentence sales pitch here for why we should study worldviews as many may ask why the police need to be able to identify worldviews today. This is simply because this is an easy way to see how some really weird thought processes actually manifest in society.

Virtues are somewhat similar to "good character" although **good character** seems to indicate the **manifestation of** the virtues in a person, meaning that the **virtues** *are the inner beliefs* of the person and **character** is how *these inner beliefs are practiced and displayed.* Others may define these differently, but these will be our benchmarks for our discussions.

Some Additional Definitions

Honor, as previously defined, is like the old handshake scenario. "He is a man of his word." Honor, of course, is the root word for honesty. By saying he is an honorable person, it means he fulfills his promises.

Creed is a brief authoritative formula (statement) of belief, often a religious belief (the Apostle's Creed or the Nicene Creed). It typically summarizes the important parts of a belief system into a short narrative. In our practical police environment, this can be a vision or mission statement or code of ethics or a department code of professional responsibility, a worthwhile thing for any department.

Valor, as previously defined, encompasses not only physical bravery *but also **moral bravery and toughness*** (for our purposes) as this is the type of scenario most likely to confront police in the immediate years to come.

Righteousness is acting in accord with divine or moral law. This is an ongoing process.

Justification means the act, process, or state of being justified by God. **Grace** is often associated with this. Grace is **unearned** mercy. The grace concept is important for law enforcement as well as religions.

I will further distinguish the terms righteousness and justification, for our purposes, by saying that **righteousness** is something *we as men attempt to attain* whereas **justification** is awarded/given *by* God. These concepts will be highlighted near the end of our discussions.

The terms I have identified above are often not widely understood, or they have a meaning that is somewhat of a surprise, like our circular definitions. That is why I noted them here. There are, of course, many other terms that deal with these moral and ethical concepts that are generally understood by the public (integrity, fidelity, courage, etc.) which we shall also use. Even with just these few concepts, we will have more than enough to get us started.

Virtue – How This Concept Will Be Badly Needed in the Very Near Future

In our last several chapters, we talked about the specific mechanical things that a profession needs to self-perpetuate itself, e.g., an organization to represent the profession, a professional journal to keep its members united and informed, commonly agreed upon standards, etc.

Then we discussed how an academy's curriculum should be modified to emphasize these mechanical elements, so that departments harvest officers *who are prepared* to accept the professional standards that *the department* will attempt to infuse into those officers for the rest of their careers.

We next will focus on those areas that are important individually for the *profession's members.* There are, of course, some overlapping areas between the mechanical and the character aspects for practitioners. For instance, the need for a vision statement was listed in the mechanical elements. In these next chapters, we will discuss what should actually go into a vison statement that is obviously more akin to morals and virtues than what we have discussed to this point. We will also focus on what specific worldviews say on these. As you can now see, we are taking several of these concepts and further refining them as we progress through this book. So, let us now apply some of these virtues in a practical way.

Universal Attributes vs. Department Initiatives

Some of the previously mentioned mechanical attributes of a profession can be accomplished by individuals and departments, e.g., recruiting good candidates, exercising good discipline, presenting relevant in-service training, etc. Others must be accomplished through academy training. Academy curriculum changes are, of course, beyond what the average officer or department can accomplish individually. That will take some planning and work. This next critical group of standards, however, can be accomplished through individual officers or departments. So, let's see what they are.

Departmentalized Canons of Conduct: We will start with this strange creature as it is nearly extinct in modern society. Most officers have not ever heard of such a thing. We previously said that *canons of conduct* are usually thought of as being above the SOP (Standard Operating

Procedure) level, and therefore, just above what departments traditionally establish. By contrast, SOPs are certainly things that departments ordain. However, we in law enforcement, do not generally have a professional organization (at least in many states) that acts as a peer review group to establish our canons of conduct state wide. Some POST organizations come close, discussed below. As previously mentioned, the Catholic Church uses such a system. It calls these overarching rules "canon law." These laws apply to Catholic Churches and priests everywhere, in Germany as well as in Canada, South America, Sweden, and Australia.

If you are in a state that does not have an entity that does this (usually manifested in a committee on **Best Practices**, or in a recognized group of **Subject Matter Experts**, for instance), I am going to suggest that individual departments ***can and should*** do this through a couple of intermediate-level committees and statements of intent. These statements, no matter what name is attached to them, help plug that huge gap between a profession-wide code of ethics (like the IACP Code of Ethics) and your department SOPs.

These can be titled something like ***The Smithville Police Department Code of Professional Responsibilities*** or ***The Jonesville Police Department Canons of Conduct*** or ***The Westville Protocol of Ideals*** or ***The Mayberry P.D.'s Creed of Beliefs***. Such a recitation summarizes these ethical ideals into easy-to-understand overviews for *officers and citizens*. They can include statements like: ***No citizen will be subjected to any unreasonable use of force by a department officer***. Several SOPs may then, of course, define specifically prohibited actions. A committee of firearms instructors (subject matter experts) could prescribe standards for when a sidearm can or should be drawn. Such standards can also be partly expressed in a department vision statement, mission statement, directive, an "intent" statement at the beginning of an SOP, or even a ***Listing of Professional Principles***. Such a vision statement may say something like: ***The Plainland Police Department will rigorously adhere to all Constitutional limitations of authority to ensure***

the maximum freedom of its citizens and visitors to our city, and to enhance our community's vitality and desirability. The name given to such a document is not important. Establishing a set of principles is!

Writing Vision and Mission Statements

A vision statement is usually a statement showing that the department is striving for a righteous department-wide professional goal, perhaps just a little beyond where the department is at now. A mission statement, perhaps even a mission statement for each of the several divisions within the department, can state what that division is accomplishing when everything is going correctly. For instance, the detective bureau, the patrol division, the jail, the warrant section, and the command section likely all have slightly different noble purposes, each requiring a different mission statement.

A mission statement for the jail section may be something like: ***All inmates will be treated with respect and not touched except when touching or force is necessary to facilitate a lawful order.*** Two or three "objectives" might also be included under the mission statement to further refine these standards.

Shared Responsibility

The medical establishment is somewhat in the same position as law enforcement in that the states have established licensing authorities that share or nearly monopolize this "standards" responsibility. If a doctor does something grossly wrong, the state revokes the doctor's license to practice. Nevertheless, the professional organization, the AMA, may still establish standards. For instance, the AMA might say that this or that elective surgery is improper if a person has this or that condition which makes that elective surgery too dangerous. There is a sharing of responsibility between the state and the professional organization.

The same sort of structure has been established in many states for law enforcement. There is a licensing or certification board that can suspend or revoke a license or certification for misbehavior, failure to maintain continuing education hours, and those sorts of things. Nonetheless, many of these states do not get down to ordaining what we have identified above as *best practices* or *accepted protocols*, i.e., canons of conduct. When they don't, **the department should!**

Is holding a cuffed arrestee down with your knee on his neck for an extended period of time acceptable practice? If so, under what circumstances? The clear direction of my thought process should jump out at you. For those who wonder if this extra effort in establishing professional standards is really worthwhile, does a multi-million-dollar lawsuit and extended federal intervention in your department make this seem more worthwhile?

Because of our recent history, this example is kind of a blinding flash of the obvious, although some departments require a brighter flash than others to motivate them [snarky and somewhat insulting, but no apology this time]. Many officers and administrators have never even considered such intermediate standards. For department administrators who do not want to generate an SOP for every conceivable situation (even if they could) overview statements on use of force, for example, are worthwhile. The question is: should we be proactive or just reactive for such high-liability situations?

Going Deeper

Since we are now moving deeper into those areas that will make for a truly professional department and great officers, we need to look at a few of the relevant virtues that have deeper meanings than most people realize. These include some terms that people often use on a superficial level but require a little more explanation to be really understood for our purposes. For our next step, these examinations will include the virtues of **justice**, **gallantry**, and **righteousness.** You will see these virtues repeatedly popping up for the rest of this book.

Critical Virtues for Law Enforcement

(Justice vs. Fairness–Preference, Equity and Other Grand Misconceptions)

What is Justice; A Practical Definition –

Justice is an *important concept* today because the modern media has focused so heavily on fairness and equity (not equality) in modern times that there is practically never any real discussion on the concept of justice. As previously mentioned, in its simplest and most direct form, justice is an eye for an eye and a tooth for a tooth, not an eye for two eyes or a tooth for half a tooth. True justice is precise.

We previously warned that the distinction between justice and fairness must be recognized. A corrupt or improper thought process in this area will very much erode the concept of *the nobility of the profession* for officers. The eye for an eye concept, of course, talks of ultimate justice. So, what should the police officer on the street be required to do?

Perhaps the most important thing about the concept of justice for street officers today is that they should not **1**) confuse justice with fairness (an easy mistake to make). The other two corruptions of the justice principle are **2**) giving preference and **3**) applying the concept of equity (as defined today) to street situations. We will addressed these last two issues shortly. For now, the first of these involves the fairness concept.

Justice vs. Fairness: The problem for officers today is that *if* they get caught up in the schism of "fairness," they always feel like they are doing wrong. Is it fair that he arrests a young person for theft who has no father-figure in the home, is poor, was surrounded by gang members, has a lower I.Q., lives mostly on the street, and is told by his mother to steal for his survival, in comparison to a privileged rich kid who was caught (arrested) for stealing an item, just for kicks, and is never formally charged? No, it is not fair, but **the arrest is just!** We must learn the difference between fairness and justice.

There will always be fairness problems in any action any human takes. One cannot avoid it. If an Affirmative Action program gets a kid into college, is it fair to a better qualified kid that he is excluded, to make room for the affirmative action applicant? Fairness is mostly a manmade emotional concept that can be twisted a thousand different ways. Justice and grace are moral concepts, precise and specific.

An eye-for-an-eye sounds very harsh from our modern-day perspective. Nonetheless, there is nothing the matter with pairing **grace** with justice, but an idea that *the violation* ***was not really*** a violation ***as is inferred*** *in the fairness perspective* is very dangerous! Fairness is a standard that often sneaks in without the officer really even realizing it. It eats away at the nobility of the profession. Grace is ***undeserved*** mercy, emphasis on the word "undeserved!" The violation really occurred and *punishment* ***is justified***, but grace may be given either by the officer or the judge.

Preference Given: The second problem area given here as a stumbling block to justice is the practice of giving preference, meaning, for instance, arresting and prosecuting conservatives for violations but not liberals for those same types of violations. Think Portland during 2020 and then the January 6th riot. This seemingly simple term can involve some deep thought processes when using it in a law enforcement context. There are, in fact, times when preference should or must be given—diplomatic immunity, for instance—but, showing preference is generally a ***terrible practice***! We will not expound on that here because it can get very technical. Nevertheless, this practice of partisanship is becoming a very real problem in today's society. Some law enforcement agencies are already heavily involved in this practice; think: the FBI and Hunter Biden. Giving preference to certain people or groups generally destroys justice. Speaking of preference, this is a great segue to the concept of equity.

Applying Current *Equity* Principles: Do not confuse "equity" with "equality." Equality speaks of equal opportunity, meaning everybody has an equal or nearly equal opportunity at a goal. Equity refers to equal outcomes. When applied to economics, this is a socialist or communist concept. This means that everybody gets the same paycheck regardless of how hard they work or how smartly they work. This is the opposite of what equality means. Equality says that everyone should have an equal opportunity to succeed (and make lots of money).

In law enforcement, an equity decision might mean that a person is not arrested because he is a black man regardless of what evidence there is that he committed a serious crime. If there have already been many blacks, for instance, arrested for that offense, the rest should not be arrested in order to keep the numbers about equal. Using current equity principles is by definition unjust. Here are two more somewhat ambiguous terms, gallantry and righteousness, that we will further define in even more detail for our purposes.

Gallantry –

This ancient concept specifically dealt with how to treat females (Merriam-Webster), but it is actually much more. We should realize that this ancient-sounding word is not used much today and is, not surprisingly, more comprehensive than modern-day man typically realizes. Using Dictionary.com, we see it also means noble-minded behavior, dashing courage, and heroic bravery. Wow, that is pretty impressive. Using Merriam-Webster's Thesaurus, we see that synonyms often used include: daringness and intrepidness. These sound somewhat like the definitions we assign to courtesy and valor, only with a little more flare and sophistication. We will, in fact, assign the concept of gallantry as being part of the term courtesy in our "Chivalry Template" in Chapter 12.

Righteousness –

Why is this virtue a mainstay? It sounds like a term the religious community uses but no one else. The importance of this virtue is that it embodies a ***constant aiming*** towards the core moral virtues, with the emphasis on the word constant. It is initiated by man because of his relationship with God, not because worldly forces entice him to act in this or that noble way. Worldly forces often do just the opposite. A person's vow (one-sided) is the motivation for noble action, not the exchange of good for good from some worldly source. Again, this is a moral mindset, and that is why it is important.

Preparing for the Near Future

We have recently received a rather good education (an almost prophetic vision) on how our elected leaders will act and react in a severe crisis in the future. What a shocking eye-opener this was in the 2020-2021 crises on the one hand, and a true blessing on the other! We now know how draconian many of our leaders can become. We now know how shortsighted they can be. We now know how overreaching they are. Those who *actually factored in* the many competing negative elements—economic collapse, stunting child development and education, instilling crippling fear, overreaction and overreach with law enforcement—were our real heroes and leaders, though few they were! They discerned what is meant by the imperfect "greatest good" principle, Chapter 11.

We have lost that depth of wisdom to a large extent over our years of prosperity and now think everything should always be a perfect one solution crisis. My father's generation possessed the wisdom of the *greatest good* philosophy and the *human nature* shortcomings because they lived through the Great Depression and WW II. That ultimately created the "Greatest Generation." Their parents had similar experiences from living through WW I. Noticing this is why a cursory study of worldviews is important for law enforcement today. This may be one of the few ways to re-instill this element of wisdom into our culture rather than waiting for an extended series of extreme catastrophes—what we used to call the school of hard-knocks—which we will undoubtedly see in the next five to seven years.

This generation of officers will undoubtedly need to rely on training to reveal these values and virtues as we are still living—even after two years of COVID—mostly in a state of *naiveté*. So, here are some virtue issues to consider ***for the next crisis***.

Perspective is Everything: Things go well when everything is going well. It is the trial that exposes the true nature of a man and mankind. Have we witnessed the near-total disregard by governmental executives during the last crisis for certain Constitutional rights like freedom of assembly, speech, and religion? An important question surfaces: Did we elect our government executives to be tyrannical dictators at the first possible excuse or to be the protectors of our Constitutional rights as best they can?

The truth is now clear on what course many or our elected leaders will again take when the opportunities present themselves. Also becoming clear is that these incidents of rebellion, e.g., the Portland riots, the Minneapolis burnings, etc., will not be just a flash in the pan and then over. These have been planned for a long time. Unfortunately, we in law enforcement will need to prepare for a rather long but exciting—if you are into that, and many officers are—series of engagements. In such an environment, a police officer on the street may well become the full extent of the protection government can extend to its citizens. Did the business owners or citizens even get that minimum level of protection in Portland or in Minneapolis in 2020?

So, what are the specific challenges in America as our social fabric continues to be torn? One important internal problem seems to be collegiality. We know that our elected leaders will likely be placing officers in untenable situations. What if we, likewise, experience no support from our fellow officers, either? Consider the below issues.

Peer Support

Collegiality in a Practical Way: A lack of collegiality in some departments is a problem. Beyond a basic knowledge that an officer's duties are morally just, another important and perhaps an even more powerful reason for teaching these attributes will be to give an officer a feeling that he is part of something bigger than himself, a band of brothers, one in a collegial relationship, someone who, along with others, champions a noble cause. He has become a member of a professional association. It should be noticed that these officers then tend to become fellow officer supportive.

Recommendation: Administrators should incorporate concepts like morals, ethics, chivalry, valor, collegiality, and the like into department vision and mission statements, canons of conduct, and other statements of belief. Such concepts, when presented at an academy, are remembered for the exam and then forgotten. Officers hopefully spend twenty-plus years at a department, not in an academy. New officers need to be shown *by the department* that the department insists on these virtues. It is hard to do this if not one virtue is ever mentioned at the department [not so subtle sarcasm]. Administrators should make these concepts an integral part of the department's core values and continuing education plan. They should train on these virtues, document them, expect them, and ***reward them*** in annual employee evaluations.

Recommendation: When creating these canons of conduct, visions statements, etc., for the department, these can simply be written by a senior staff member but a better approach might be establishing these through a roundtable (peer) discussion (like the template outlined in Chapter 12) or a committee on professional standards (with members from all levels within the department or perhaps even with a few outsiders like merit commission members, community leaders, religious leaders, etc.). Contributions to these standards can also come from a *committee of best practices* or any number of *committees of subject matter experts*. This will encourage buy-in with the officers, demonstrate that the department is serious in these matters, and speak to the public as well.

Discussions on Some Worldviews

In a chapter devoted to identifying "Virtue, Character, Nobility, and Other Really Abstract Ideas," we will conclude with a few short paragraphs on the subject of worldviews. We will eventually devote an entire chapter to discussing worldviews, Chapter 11. This subject would naturally fit and be placed right here except that it is so large.

There Are Some "Bad" Worldviews: Worldviews are a consolidation of these attributes, i.e., virtues, perspectives, etc., into a recognizable philosophy and are, therefore, the next logical step of inquiry after learning what attributes and virtues are. I know that many will ask, why in the world would officers need any training today in worldviews? They are neither professors of philosophy nor church pastors nor Vatican officials. This need is a practical one. This need is simply because these worldviews are how ***actual groups*** in our society present to the police. Today we have Wiccans, Satanists, Illuminati, Marxists, Naturalists, Secular Humanists and hundreds of other recognized views openly practicing in our society. Some of these are not good for law enforcement or society. Some are actually dangerous!

There Are Some "Good" Worldviews: So, officers should be able to at least recognize the types of problems that a particular group is likely to present. Officers should also recognize the admirable attributes (virtues) that got America from 1776 to 2022. By exposing new officers to those belief systems, we might provide a better foundation upon which they can build their careers. Without a grasp on why officers are putting themselves on the line, officers are likely to eventually ask: What am I doing here? Is this worth it? Why should I be putting myself at risk for that? They need to have an ethical underpinning and a moral overview to answer these questions.

Why is this introduction to worldviews presented here rather than at the beginning of Chapter 11 where these worldviews are going to be primarily discussed? Because I would ask you to think about what virtues and which worldview elements are the ***most needed*** for today's officers.

Everybody, EVERYBODY complains about high turnover rates and substandard performance and insufficient preparation of our new officers, but not many give these problems much deep thought or attempt to discern what these new officers *really need* to help correct these deficiencies. Hopefully, by the time you arrive at Chapter 11, you will bring a few of these solutions to our discussions. This is not rocket science, but it does require more than two minutes of contemplation [snarky at an almost undetectable level].

What Next?

In this chapter, we presented the 30,000-foot view of what seemed like a hundred and one topics. I mentioned at the very start of this chapter that this chapter would be a mega-chapter. If you now have a headache, we understand. You have undoubtedly noticed by now that this chapter was not a full or detailed lesson on virtues. That is reserved for your in-service curriculum. As you can see, this book is not the *Complete Guide to Police Ethics*, it is *The **Little** ... **Book*** ... It is your starting point. It is your reservoir of MANY worthwhile topics for your department training calendar for the next ten, perhaps twenty, years [maybe that is a little optimistic].

So, if worldviews are going to be pushed off for several chapters, what is next? Well, we will next begin focusing on some *very specific* real-world problems which are likely to manifest in the next couple of years in our chapter COVID 1984. After that, we will talk about the ultra-important issue of an officer's **1938 Moment**. ❖

Chapter 8

COVID-1984 and Beyond

(Some Really Practical Applications)

I heard a religious commentator, Jan Markell, use the tongue-in-cheek label "COVID-1984" a few years ago, and I thought it appropriate. We are now seeing the scenarios mentioned in the book *Nineteen Eighty-Four* coming to life, before our eyes. The progression of these scenarios will only increase in frequency and intensity, much like birth pangs. We in law enforcement do not have a choice whether to allow these to manifest or not (Bible prophecy always comes to pass), only whether to prepare for them or not.

In this chapter and the next, we will identify a few additional problems that surfaced during our last crises in 2020 and 2021, and what the (often undesirable) reactions were for law enforcement. We will then anticipate what may happen in the near future as these types of things get even more severe. We will do this by looking at developing worldviews and news events. We will then devote an entire chapter to the Judeo-Christian ethos and explain why we think this worldview is the gold standard for police officers.

Three Critical Areas: But first, let us look at one of the challenges we faced in 2020 and 2021: **abusive decrees.** We will also discuss two additional areas of conflict which easily could develop out of highly abusive decrees. These two: the **suspension of the writ of habeas corpus** and **martial law**, may seem unlikely to some, but then the COVID lockdowns, masking, social distancing, and decree overreach seemed unlikely to most in 2019. But first, let us look at "emergency" (a.k.a., abusive) decrees.

Decrees

To start our discussion on decrees, we must, as always, define the terms. You are probably getting tired of hearing me say this, but it is so important in this age where the radical Left is attempting to change the meanings of so many concepts and words. Along this line, we sometimes hear the words edicts, declarations, proclamations, commands, discretionary orders, regulations, and the like being used in these situations. When searching the dictionary, we again find that circular definition problem with "edict" and other such terms. Consequently, we will simply stick with the word *decree* for all of those terms in our discussions.

Our composite definition for the word decree, combining several dictionary definitions, is: ***An order given by a single person or group that has the force of law***. The scary part about this is that the executive is not usually required to satisfy any kind of threshold justification for such a decree to an outside authority before imposing it, although there are sometimes limitations on duration, scope, etc., written in some of those emergency statutes.

Luckily, several state supreme courts have stepped in with decisions in 2020 and 2021, proclaiming that those defendant-executives had substantially exceeded their power and that the Constitution is not nullified by a decree. Mayors, governors, health officers, and other executives are generally allowed by statute to issue these decrees in America for short periods of time when an "emergency" occurs. The problem comes in defining both a short period of time and an emergency.

Again, The Proper Perspective: As mentioned, these decrees do not suspend our Constitutional system, at least in theory. But what if a decree is used to close down churches when liquor stores, big box stores, bars, strip clubs, marijuana shops or houses of prostitution (where legal) are not closed? Has the First Amendment right to practice our religions been violated? Even though executives may not be "believers" and may absolutely hate religious pronouncements, they are still bound by the Constitution. One should notice that religious freedom is *specifically protected* in the Constitution, but protections for liquor stores, houses of prostitution, and marijuana shops are not.

Further compounding the problem is that initiating the decree procedure can be a very fast process. A governor can declare an emergency, issue a decree, and have it promulgated throughout a state in a matter of hours. Compare that to the normal legislative process where counter arguments are allowed. Some of these decrees are civil in nature (enforced only through court order or fine), but some have the force of criminal law that can justify arrest and, upon conviction, a jail sentence. As mentioned, an important point about an emergency decree is that these do not generally void other laws or the Constitution, e.g., the writ of habeas corpus, for instance.

What Actually Happened: Nevertheless, the stories reported in the media in 2020 of executives—and consequently, then the police—overstepping their authority numbered in the hundreds, if not thousands, in communities clear across the country. To a certain degree, this is understandable as we were not accustomed to handling these situations. Unfortunately, these resulted in some *very bad* PR for law enforcement. These created the perfect storm for the "Defund-the-Police" movement, largely successful from a radical Left perspective, and the revoke-their-qualified-immunity efforts, not so successful yet, as well as a bunch of police reform bills. Law enforcement's moment of naivety should now be past!

Police should now be considering to what degree they will be willing to allow themselves to be used to enforce highly abusive, partisan, unconstitutional, illegal, or immoral decrees in the future. The hope—by many, including many police administrators—is that we will return to the "old normal," and we will not have to worry about such decisions in the future. It should now be obvious, however, that the old-normal is never going to return. This contention is not only supported by the real-world events caused by Joe Biden's many executive orders—huge inflation, massive spending, food shortages, bungled military withdrawal, 87,000 new IRS agents, etc.—but also by end-time Bible prophecy. I would suggest that police administrators who do not prepare their departments for such coming events are truly derelict in their duties.

Recommendation: Police administrators need to review these recent *First Amendment and Second Amendment court cases* and those yet to be finally adjudicated, and incorporate those decisions into in-service training schools, within relevant policy statements, and perhaps even into vision statements and mission statements. This is critical for guiding officers in these uncertain areas in the future, even in hot button subjects like the writ of habeas corpus. For those who think writing policy concerning the writ of habeas corpus is unneeded, I would ask those administrators to do some research. The suspension of the writ actually sprang up ***on both sides*** of the political spectrum early in our 2020-2021 confrontations. Really? Yes!

Suspension of The Writ of Habeas Corpus

About halfway between the emergency decree and the full imposition of martial law is the status of citizens being subject to or confined under the legal suspension of the writ of habeas corpus. Any discussion of this issue seemed a totally ridiculous and worthless dialogue in December of 2019 or before. That could never happen here in America, could it? Well, it, in fact, was actually proposed by U.S. Attorney General William Barr (a man who I previously admired) at the very beginning of the 2020 riots. Luckily, the political inclination of our President then did not support this.

Hopefully, those in law enforcement are not so naïve today. The fact is that President Abraham Lincoln (who I admire) did—along with declaring martial law throughout the South when it was obvious that we were heading into a long civil war—suspend the writ as one of his first acts in the war. Chief Justice Taney of the U.S. Supreme Court then declared Lincoln's decree on the suspension of the writ unconstitutional. Lincoln then simply ignored Taney's decision for the entire Civil War.

Some More History: To give some background, this writ is an old English common law writ that was incorporated into our Constitution that gave, and still gives, citizens the right to have the reason for their arrest and confinement reviewed by a civilian court of law. We specifically incorporated that principle into our Constitution, Article 1, Section 9, because it is so central to our ideas of liberty, fairness, and freedom.

This writ also involves a number of very important ancillary rights. In short, as far as law enforcement is concerned, suspension of the writ allows government officials, i.e., the police, to apprehend *and confine* citizens indefinitely without due process. Think internment camps—already suggested by both sides, but for vastly different reasons—during the 2020 riots and after the 2021 election. Besides Bill Barr's request, claims were made in early 2021 that we should have anti-vaxxer camps and re-education camps for "Trumpers," and there were, in fact, legislative proposals in both New York and Washington state for anti-vaxxer camps, see footnote #6, Chapter 1.

Our WW II Example: If one still thinks that this could never happen here, a massive example involved the internment of Japanese-Americans during WW II. Yes, history is a great teacher! There was a fear among military commanders and then the general population at the start of WW II on the west coast that those of Japanese ancestry might initiate contacts with Japanese nationals unless they were isolated. Does the use of this fear element sound familiar? Many undesirable things can happen in a time of fear.

Most of those Japanese-Americans were U.S. citizens whose families had been here for generations. Military and police [did I just say, "***and police?***"] snatched them out of their homes and businesses. Many lost everything. The U.S. Supreme Court, years later, found such internment orders to be improper without directly overruling the procedure, but that certainly did not help those Japanese-Americans at the time.

The last of those internment camps was closed just slightly over three years before this author was born. In fact, there are thousands of Americans who are still alive today who were in the military or were policemen when those apprehensions were made, so this *is not* ancient history. But that couldn't happen today, could it?

Why weren't the Japanese-Americans on the east coast rounded up? Some point out that this was simply because the east coast was within a different military district, and under a different commanding general, who apparently did not think this necessary (or perhaps moral). That does not sound like equal protection for all, but of course, that was wartime and people were scared.

Along this line, former President Obama made a campaign promise that he was going to close Guantanamo Bay (a POW camp) because most of those detainees (POWs, prisoners of war) had been there for years (the war on terror) without a single charge being filed against most of them. That campaign promise was never satisfied.

This POW camp involved mostly foreign "combatants," apprehended in foreign lands, and never brought physically into the United States. Although these confinements were done under the War Powers Act, the confinements are for an indefinite period of time (usually until the declaration of war is lifted by the Congress, which has never happened). This was not a direct result of the suspension of the writ, but it is very similar and instructive for police.

The important point for law enforcement is that once these powers are implemented, they are ***very slow** to be rescinded*! This power, if implemented, will certainly result in a rather important conscience consideration for officers in the future. We will talk about an officer's "**1938 Moment**" in some detail in our next chapter.

Potential for Internment Camps Today –

After Joe Biden's inauguration, I was really surprised that he did not condemn the call for "re-education camps." That really says something! So, the question becomes: If everyone just ignores the Constitution and Constitutional violations, do we really have a Constitution? More importantly for the police is the question: What do such camps mean for the law enforcement profession?

How many officers would be in favor of placing parents, neighbors, relatives, friends, and pastors in internment camps for refusing to take a vaccine or for political reasons or for their religious views or for voicing an opinion at a school board meeting or for being a member of a pro-life organization, or for …? The next obvious question for officers is: How could officers resist enforcing illegal decrees and still keep their jobs? Police administrators should not ignore the possibility that this could happen. The ramifications are huge, and the time to think about this is now.

Governors and Mayors: Governors and mayors will also need to confront this new political reality in order to decide if they are going to command their police departments to enforce those overreaching, draconian orders. To answer our previous question, if such internment camps are ever established, officers will likely be tasked with apprehending certain identifiable groups, *en masse*, and taking them to POW-like camps without a court order or review. Even without the writ being suspended, we have several people from the "January 6th Riot" who reportedly are still confined, at the time of this writing, in the D.C. jails awaiting trial, in segregation (a nice word for solitary confinement), more than a year after the riot.

Recommendation: This is ***a really important recommendation***! ***Please consider it fully.*** If a vision and mission statement are developed as well as a number of good canons of conduct, officers have a much easier time refusing to enforce obviously unconstitutional, abusive, illegal, or immoral decrees. Mayors also have a more difficult time asking officers to enforce these obviously illegal and unconstitutional orders when they have ***previously*** *bought into* these higher ethical standards.

Such statements of higher ethical conduct may very well be ***the best protection officers will have*** when their "1938 Moment" arrives. For this reason, all departments are encouraged to create these statements of ethical propriety. They are more than just the next step in the professionalization process. They may very well become the bulwark for retaining and maintaining good officers and standards in tough times.

On a personal level, officers can resist, psychologically, the pressure to enforce obviously unethical orders easier if they accept a personal moral code and worldview, and are part of a collegial (professional) association that has a code. Colleagues reinforce colleagues! Being the Lone Ranger is not so easy in these situations.

Martial Law

Martial law certainly could not happen here in the U.S., could it? Many would have said this prior to former President Trump's house being searched by the FBI. It is now obvious the Left is hoping for an arrest to keep him from running in 2024. When this happens, perhaps the likelihood of protests, disturbances and riots, and then martial law, becomes more of a reality.

We will only briefly discuss martial law here. We now have the experience, hopefully, to realize that things can flare towards a surprisingly quick domestic upheaval. Internationally, we now know how quickly the Ukraine situation manifested. Might we also be near a WW III situation? Think: the Russia-Ukraine conflict, China-Taiwan, and Ezekiel 38. Those of us living during the Bay of Pigs realize how quickly those nuclear confrontations materialize. Those living during Pearl Harbor also realized this. Most Americans in 2019 did not ever contemplate this possibility.

Abuse Likely: Martial law is the final and most extreme step in this progression, but not completely out of the realm of possibility today. Some leftist areas of the world like China and North Korea totally shut down huge cities, even in late 2022, by simple decree. Another somewhat liberal area, the EU, came very close to martial law during the COVID crisis by just using emergency decrees. In a bona fide declaration of martial law, unless limited by orders from a military superior, military officers are given huge amounts of authority while operating under this jurisdiction. That, of course, does not make everything they do morally okay. Actually, it is just the opposite for a moral, virtue-filled officer. Instances of abuse are very likely under such a declaration.

Martial law is imposed (domestically) when the rule of law in society has broken down to such an extent that only military intervention will restore order. When martial law is declared, the military commander in that area is all-powerful. His orders not only subject military members to his will but also civilians. In such a situation, suspension of other civil laws as well as Constitutional protections are possible. During such periods, civilians are tried in military tribunals (if tried at all) for violating an order. They are then confined in a military-style brig or stockade, or internment camp. But why is this important to local police officers?

Will Local Police Be Involved?: Local police officers might say that these jurisdictions are military authorities, and they will not have any part in these actions, but if a large portion of the country would go under martial law, it is not likely that the military would have enough personnel to be able to administer every city and town. Local officers will probably find themselves called upon to fill the gaps. If one has ever watched the movie *Casablanca*—depicting a story during the WW II era—one may have noticed how the civilian (French) police commander was really just an extension of German authority.

If officers ever find themselves either in a state-imposed or a nationally-imposed martial law situation, their authority will likely be increased exponentially. The real issue for civilian police officers then is how they will treat citizens in such a situation. The mechanics of operating under such authority will not be discussed here as this is a less likely scenario, at least for now, and more dependent upon the military commander's whim than on an established set of procedures.

Just remember, there was the equivalent of martial law imposed throughout the South during the U.S. Civil War, and it was in effect from 1860 to 1865, not an inconsequential period of time. The current U.S. Insurrection Act actually has provisions for imposing U.S. military authority *within* the United States. Hopefully, things will not come to this.

The First Freedoms

We will insert a rather lengthy but important section here after the decree, internment, and martial law sections having to do with our First Freedoms. These are the ones that abusive decrees, internment camps, and martial law seem to target the most in a practical sense. Fortunately, we have not yet arrived at the point at which martial law or the suspension of the writ of habeas corpus has been imposed, but we have, regrettably, already arrived at one serious Constitutional crossroad, the First Amendment's rights to the freedom of religion, freedom of assembly, and freedom of speech being purposely and totally ignored by many governmental executives.

Beyond the United States, stories of overzealous world leaders developing a gestapo mentality became pretty common in the coronavirus pandemic, undoubtedly the result of WEF influence and training. As mentioned, one of the most conspicuous confrontations has been between these executives and churches.

Still More History: Our Founding Fathers all had *direct* and *personal* experience with tyranny, oppressive decrees, and martial law in those pre-revolutionary days. Those experiences explain the deliberate and specific inclusion of the "first freedoms" into the Constitution which were, in theory, the *supreme law* of the land. With our recent experiences, those rights do not seem nearly as supreme today. We have already posed the question: If we pay no attention to the Constitution, do we really have a Constitution? Do we really need a federal court to issue a court order before we stand for Constitutional provisions?

The Supreme Law of the Land: It is important to note that the Founding Fathers placed these protections in the Constitution because *they had experienced those tyrannies,* and they, consequently, elevated these principles to be above ordinary law, to be the supreme law of the land, not to be subordinated to the despotic decrees of powermongers.

While teaching at the academy, I always had several hours with the new chiefs while they were completing their "chiefs' school." I routinely warned them that they may be confronted with deciding between enforcing an unconstitutional, illegal, unethical, or immoral order given to them by the mayor or losing their chief's position (job).

In discussing this quandary with the chiefs at their roundtable class, someone would always say that if they did not enforce the order, they would be out of a job and the next person would be faced with exactly the same situation, and the mayor would eventually find someone who would issue the order. This, of course, is absolutely true. I never thought that I would see the day when line officers would be facing such a decision for decree declarations. For line officers, the ramifications are highly impactful. A line officer can (probably will) lose his job, will have to finance all appeals personally (unless he has some type of insurance to pay for legal representation), and will endure a long series of court battles before his good name is re-established, if ever.

Jeopardy for Officers Enforcing an Unconstitutional Decree

As noted, a line officer may lose his job if *he refuses* to enforce such an order, but he may also be subjecting himself and the city to liability for a false arrest or excessive use of force claim *if he enforces the order*. As mentioned, decrees do not automatically void all previous constitutional protections given to citizens. Someone suing eighteen months after an incident may allege that Constitutional and established state statutory law (passed by the legislature) supersedes the "decree law" of a municipality's executive. How much training have officers had on conflicts of law, meaning when the wording of a decree conflicts with a state statute or U.S. Constitutional provision? None!

Will Officers Be Personally Liable? – Qualified Immunity: Of course, an officer (or his attorney) would then allege that a Constitutional standard had not been clearly established—the requirement for a claim of qualified immunity—so that he is not *personally liable* for such a violation. This, of course, does not exempt him from the court case, even if immunity is granted. The workings of that provision of the law are too involved to discuss right here, but can one see how complicated this can become? We will revisit this legal concept a little later. Nevertheless, might it be better to think about these things *before* we are in the midst of the fray? We are definitely plowing new ground here, and preparing officers is critical.

A Quick Comparison; The Established and the New –

When we say that we are plowing new ground, the paramilitary police services are a relatively new component of our society compared to military organizations. The military law of orders is well developed (the UCMJ in America) in comparison to our law enforcement systems. This will be a time when our need for good procedure will be more important than any other time in history. We truly now need a system that supports and preserves good officers.

Military and Police – Disobeying an Order: I promised a comparison. In short, the practical differences between a civilian police officer refusing an order are substantially different than a military member refusing an order. Procedures for handling this situation in the military have developed over many centuries. Even though a military member refusing an order can subject himself to conviction of a military offense with some potential for extended incarceration, this rarely is the case for a first offense.

Even with a court-martial—rather than an "Article-15," a non-judicial proceeding—military justice procedures entitle the military member to a review of the alleged violation by a court-martial board which has officers who understand what an "illegal" order is. And a soldier, unlike a civilian policeman, continues to receive his paycheck during the proceedings and has a lawyer appointed to him at no expense to him. His family members also retain their status as dependents (for commissary purposes as well as their housing benefit) until there is a conviction.

If the solder is convicted, he has a right to a substantial appeal process through others who know what an illegal order is. Unless an involuntary discharge is imposed as part of the sentence, the soldier again becomes employed as a regular military member when his stockade time is completed, meaning he still has a career. Not so with a police officer.

A police officer who disobeys an order is usually *fired immediately* and, of course, loses his paycheck. He must hire an attorney *at his own expense* since the proceeding is civil. His right to appeal his firing must be asserted and the level of proof required of the prosecuting department is only a preponderance of the evidence. Appeal fees through the courts from that termination decision are also at the *former officer's expense*, and once the termination decision is upheld, re-employment in the law enforcement sector is not ever likely. Yes, police officers have a lot riding on any decision to refuse an order, no matter how immoral an order is on its face.

Taking a Stand or Not: My purpose for this long-winded explanation is to show that civilian police officers who hold to a moral conviction will likely face some truly difficult decisions in the near future until this new area of the law begins to be developed through the courts and some norms are established. Like the Japanese internments during WW II, the pronouncement years later that this should not have happened does not help a police officer at all in the present. For enforcing much of the criminal law, officers have 240 years of court precedent upon which to rely. "Decree law" is a **whole new experience**!

Going With the Flow – Why Rock the Boat?: There are some powerful reasons for officers—in their *1938 Moment*—to just *go along and get along* with the current woke attitudes, unconstitutional decrees, or immoral orders from superiors. Like the chief who says that if he does not comply with the mayor's order, the mayor will just get someone who will, many line officers will say that their first obligation must be to bring home a paycheck for their families, and they will enforce 99.9% of all issued decrees, improper or not, rather than lose their jobs. I know that I am droning *on and on* concerning this, but it is perhaps the most important issue facing law enforcement today and is generally not recognized or is just ignored.

My point is that the system is heavily weighted towards encouraging officers to enforce decrees, a good thing, but also to enforce totally immoral decrees, a bad thing. Officers who have no concept of the virtues will likely carry out such immoral orders, and they may even relish imposing their new-found super-authority over others.

Qualified Immunity – A Very Short Explanation: We have mentioned the concept of qualified immunity a few paragraphs ago. Most civilians reading this book probably have no idea what this entails. Just as a very short explanation, qualified immunity does not shield an officer from personal liability if the right violated has been clearly shown to exist through prior court decisions. It is only applicable for new or undeveloped areas of the law. Most agree that it seems unfair to hold officers *personally* liable when there is no standard yet established. The employing entity (the department, the county, the state) will, nonetheless, be held liable if it is later found that a violation of the Constitution or statutes had occurred.

It would be easy to go off on a sidetrack concerning all of the technicalities of qualified immunity or the substantial efforts early in 2020 to do away with qualified immunity for police officers, but that is a discussion for another book. Suffice it to say that in 2020, it was *repeatedly suggested* that officers *should lose* their qualified immunity protections, and there was, in fact, a bill introduced into Congress to do just that. Nonetheless, such demands will undoubtedly materialize again if another situation were to surface of substantial police abuse. This, unfortunately, demonstrates how all of these "legal" principles and protections are oh so intertwined with politics.

Even with qualified immunity remaining intact, subjecting officers and their families to years of court proceedings, depositions, and intense media scrutiny, for alleged violations of Constitutional rights—regardless of who ultimately wins or whether immunity is ultimately granted—is just plain traumatic for officers and their families, and especially for their children.

Recommendation: First and Second Amendment Rights: As previously mentioned, all officers should receive First Amendment training—not typically presented today in basic academy law classes—and police executives should present this in the department until academies begin instructing in these areas. Some new Supreme Court decisions concerning the First and Second Amendment have already occurred and can substantially clarify these rights. Those decisions will undoubtedly stimulate other cases until these areas of the law become, as they say, settled. Until that time, First and Second Amendment rights should be a mainstay of department in-service training AND new policy statements.

The Church Question, in Particular -

As for the First Amendment, nearly all churches conformed to the decrees in the early months of the pandemic, but as standards were developed like masking and social distancing, churches began to chafe under lockdown decrees that obviously discriminated against them. Closures or limits of 15 people or less for huge cathedrals—and designations that classified them as "non-essential" while others like abortion clinics, liquor stores, marijuana shops (where legal), airlines, and even public protests (i.e., riots) were proclaimed *as essential* in many states—quickly wore on church ministers and priests. Even though many of those churches could easily satisfy masking and social distancing rules, they were highly restricted or closed. Sometimes their pastors were arrested, even in the United States.

Throughout this book, I have taken strides to present only an overview of the related issues. In this area, I went a bit deeper as I perceive this subject to be one of the most serious of our time. If First Amendment rights are ignored, do we have any hope of retaining any other rights whatsoever?

Large scale First Amendment violations have *already occurred*, as evidenced by many court decisions including several U.S. Supreme

Court decisions. In this one area, the things that ***could not possibly happen here*** in the U.S. have actually happened. We absolutely now know our leaders are capable of draconian decrees and ignoring basic Constitutional rights. I pray I have not put all of my readers into a deep coma in this chapter, but this one area, more than others, is critical for our country and its law enforcement systems.

Again, Considering the Future

In all these situations—operating under emergency decrees, suspension of the writ of habeas corpus (internment camps), or martial law—officers need to consider, substantially ahead of time, what they will do when given an order that confronts their own moral standards or a professional ethic.

They must also consider how they will *limit* ***themselves*** from imposing corrupt, illegal, abusive, or immoral orders upon subordinates and civilians in the coming era. These situations will quickly identify whether we have truly become a profession or are still only an occupation, skill, or trade without any substantial moral underpinnings. One must ask: ***How would we do under such situations tomorrow without any additional training today?*** We will pose similar questions at the end of each of the next several chapters as gauges of our professional development and progress. ❖

Chapter 9

An Officer's 1938 Moment

We are building towards a grand crescendo in this book. This crescendo will be labeled our "***1938 Moment***" and will assimilate all that we have discussed. This chapter will expose the trigger point in that effort. This is the point at which an officer makes a moral decision as to how he will handle his life and job from that moment on. It will be that moment or series of events when a profound decision *must* be made because the two alternative courses are so divergent. The officer will either go with the flow of current public opinion and culture or take a stand for what is unquestionably right. This label—the 1938 Moment—comes from the type of situation that occurred in Berlin, Germany in November of 1938. More on this a little later in the chapter, but first, as always, some background.

History and Future Shock

In the coming years, officers will likely be facing the same challenges as officers faced in the turbulent 1960s but also many new areas that officers have never faced before. As previously suggested, an even more onerous period of emergency decrees could be on the horizon because of another virus outbreak, continued civil unrest, all-out armed insurrection, "climate change" crisis, or other like reasons. Are our police officers prepared psychologically to deal with these moral dilemmas?

Most of these areas are uncharted ground for American police officers today. Like subject-specific training and officer roundtables, *canons of conduct* can really help, thus, our last couple of chapters. But now, we must anticipate more than just general challenges—like riots, premeditated burnings, food shortages, and flash lootings—that today's officers have not seen before. We must focus on that one moment when an officer will be called to make a profound decision that will likely shape his mindset from that point on.

The Moment of Truth

Using the title, "The Moment of Truth" may seem a little dramatic, but it is not. It truly will be such a moment. One of my main purposes for this book is the question: Will all of our police officers just decide to go with the flow when things start to ebb into an abusive, immoral, or unconstitutional direction? Some believe that we will never arrive at such a time, but my study of prophetic events tells me otherwise. I will not bog you down with this study. Justifying my viewpoint would take an additional book or two, so we will not go there.

Nevertheless, as officers and administrators see the subsequent waves—now getting to be tsunamis—of deterioration occurring in our society, I am hoping that at some point a few will at least decide to seriously consider what I have to say. In short, I am hoping that a substantial number of officers will resist the dreadful but easy mainstream alternatives and choose the one steeped in professional ethics and moral righteousness. The goal of this book is to provide some ethical underpinnings that officers can use to bolster their character which will, hopefully, avoid a total moral collapse of our law enforcement system.

Part of preparing for this is to reveal fully that one critical moment, that 1938 Moment, which most officers will face in this upcoming age of social chaos, deception, and corruption. As a relevant example, let us look at what actually happened in Germany in November of 1938, for some edification and possibly a little wisdom.

That 1938 Moment

Germany was still somewhat of an open western culture in the 1930s when the "**Night of Broken Glass**" occurred, at least for the mainstream. This was not the case for the Jews. I often use this example in my current promotion schools because it mirrors so closely what is happening today. Hitler came to power in 1933, not by coup d'état or military takeover, but by election. He rallied a wave of fanaticism that was truly spectacular. Inflation, economic collapse, and many social factors allowed Hitler to convince the German people that they could be successful if they would just follow him. Hitler identified German-Jews, especially bankers and businessmen, as being part of the problem for Germany's slow economic recovery after World War One.

On November 9, 1938, this fanatical wave led to "The Night of Broken Glass" in which citizens and the Sturmabteilung (a paramilitary wing of the Nazi party) marched on the Jewish district of Berlin, pulling Jews from their homes, beating them, burning their businesses, and eventually hauling them off to internment camps, which later became concentration camps, which later became death camps.

Where were the police and military during those hours, days, and months of riots, burnings, and internments? They were mostly standing by, watching all of this happen or participating in it! Of course, the German central government was all in favor of those riots. Consequently, opposing those riots had ramifications. Does this sound like the lack of decisive action that resulted in the burnings in Minneapolis and elsewhere in 2020? Does that sound like today?

What was it specifically that prevented German police from interceding to protect the Jewish population? Well, there was certainly a history of five years of increasing authoritarian rule by the Nazis. There was obviously no support from the command section of the police to do their duty. There probably was not much, if any, collegial support for protecting the Jews, either. Does that sound like today?

At that instant, all of those German police officers experienced what I have now labelled as their "***1938 Moment***." It literally then came down to an individual officer's character. Without training and discussion, what are the chances that officers will be able to withstand such pressures? We are seeing those conditions being duplicated today. There are several good lessons here for today's officers and administrators.

One Good Lesson–The Reichstag Fire: Besides googling, "The Night of Broken Glass," one should also google the "Reichstag Fire." This involved the burning of the German parliament building in Berlin in 1933, very shortly after the Nazi party took power. This was used as a justification for that government to assume "**emergency powers**" (i.e., to become a dictatorship) ***to protect the people*** *in a time of emergency.*

It was later claimed that it was actually the Nazis who started the fire in order to justify the assumption of extreme powers. Five were charged for the arson. Four were actually acquitted, which is amazing, considering that politically-charged environment of the day. This would be like trying a conservative political defendant in a Washington, D.C., court today. A 24-year-old was eventually convicted but was later fully pardoned, posthumously, in 2008. Interesting! Perhaps later generations realized he was standing before a kangaroo court.

Obviously, the Nazis knew how to use and control the media to spread the narrative they wanted. They knew how to inflame their side to violent behavior. They knew how to identify a group to hate for their problems. Sound familiar? Today, the American media is squarely behind the Left, the Left knows how to incite violence among its members, and the groups to hate in America are conservatives and Christians. Hey, that does sound familiar! [I know, sarcasm again.]

But that was not the first use of such a strategy in history against a major religious group. One should also look at how Nero justified killing all those Christians. Despotic leaders often accuse the opposition of doing exactly what they are doing. Again, sound familiar? This game plan is not new, but is often *very* successful. This lead-up period to our coming second revolution is when ***good is presented as evil*** and ***evil is presented as good***! Are we there yet? Yep, history really does tell us a lot [not sarcasm, just fact].

When WW II Was Over: When the war was over and those German commanders were asked why they committed such atrocities ***against their own citizens***, they—nearly to the person—all answered that they were just following orders. At the Nuremberg Trials, that excuse did not prove a good defense for either military personnel or the police. [Google: the Ernst Kalterbrunner case, the highest-ranking SS (police) officer to be convicted and hanged.]

The SS (or Schutzstaffel) was a national paramilitary German police unit that willingly carried out all of Hitler's edicts. Is anything like that happening in this country? Think: FBI and IRS? The question naturally surfaces with today's events progressing as they are: What will our current police officers do when they have their ***1938 Moment***?

The point to our *1938 Moment* discussion is that certain conditions in America and the world are again looking very much like they did in Germany in the 1930s. What might King Solomon have to say about this? He probably would say that history repeats itself, and if the conditions are *very* closely duplicated, we can predict ***with a high degree of accuracy*** how humans—because human nature has not changed—will react when confronted with these issues again. We will look closely at this historical paradigm in our next chapter, "History as Our Schoolmaster," but for the rest of this chapter, we will examine a few really thorny questions having to do with ***our*** 1938 moments. If we know about these conditions, will we be able to change the outcomes, at least to a small degree, this time around?

Some Thorny Questions

We will now begin to step back again for a wider view of things, both for discussing our mechanical requirements for becoming a true profession and for the individual attributes that practitioners need to display to the public to be considered true professionals. We do this to make this book practical and functional.

A Mantra: Officers on the street and administrators need some general principles that they can recite at the tip of their tongues to deal with the challenges soon to face law enforcement. These officers can at any time, if they wish, dig into this or other sources to get the nitty-gritty discussions of the differences between a moral and an ethical standard, or the technical definition of gallantry, but they also need a few overarching (quick-reference) principles to keep them on the narrow path. Each and every officer should absolutely construct his own mantra.

Linking difficult questions to an overarching theme (a mantra)—similar to what is done in the case law approach to the study of law—will be helpful to officers in connecting theory to real world practical application in the ethics area. For instance, in criminal law, the technical admonition that, "You need to Mirandize him now," is instantly recognized by all officers.

In the ethics area, this can be a saying like: ***Leaders, lead***; ***God does not call the qualified, He qualifies the called***; ***Gallantry Always***; ***Power Corrupts***; ***Discipline makes officers shine***; ***Failure to prepare is preparing to fail***; or any other self-administered admonition.

These admonitions will help when thorny questions like the following surface: *Is any method justified to restore order in a community when many citizens have been killed because of insurrection or riots, even if these methods are unconstitutional, immoral, or unethical,* i.e., ***Do the ends justify the means***, a utilitarian question, Chapter 11? Does, "I was just following orders," fly as an excuse for immoral conduct? Is "science" really a justification for internment camps for anti-vaxxers?

These all point to the usefulness of a worldview, sometimes called an ethos, and a mantra.

Other questions that surface include: If I don't go along with those decree orders, I am, of course, likely to be fired, so *should I offer* ***any*** *resistance at all* to immoral and illegal decrees? ***At what point do I take a stand?*** These are all questions that should be examined at the department level sooner, rather than later. The number of new areas of dilemma that have surfaced over the past two years are many.

Some Hot-Button Issues

As mentioned, the reason this book was written is because of these coming issues! They are all profound! Mismanagement of these issues has so many undesirable ramifications for law enforcement that we would be derelict if we did not discuss these. So, let us look at a few of the very current hot-button issues and the virtues they impact.

Are Subsequent Lockdown Orders Likely? –

If police officers were asked in November of 2019 if country-wide extended lockdown orders were likely for 2020, very few would have said that those would likely occur. If asked today if such decrees are likely for an "emergency condition" in the future, many officers would likely say, ***yes, absolutely!*** I keep reminding my readers of these two statements because this second question has some real ramifications.

Two Choices: We have aired these two choices previously and asked you to think about these. Now we will look at them for some solutions. The two above statements explain why we were not prepared to handle these situations initially. These unfortunately, resulted in some very bad consequences and PR for law enforcement in many places, e.g., defund the police, revoke police immunity laws, pass reform bills, gut departments, decimate the number of good applicants! Departments just do not prepare for *highly unlikely* situations. Nonetheless, that second statement—could this happen again?—asks a profound question for law enforcement. If we are anticipating more of these types of situations in the near future, is it not critical that we begin to prepare for these? If we don't, isn't that negligence and dereliction of duty?

This section is not meant to rehash what we have already said concerning draconian decrees or our unprepared condition in March of 2020 or our need to prepare tactically for riotous situations in the future. It is how to prepare our officers, personally and psychologically for the future. This chapter's discussion is to highlight that, YES, this **CAN likely happen again in the near future**. Therefore, let us talk in a little more detail about the practical responses for preparing our officers now: *training* and *policy responses* to these issues.

Training and Discussions Are Key to Good Police Ethics

You may be asking what does designing a future training curriculum have to do with instilling virtues within officers or professionalizing an occupation? The answer is: everything! Sure, we need to prepare for these events just because these events pose risks, but what in the world is the link between riot training, for instance, and the professionalization process?

Well, for those of us who have been involved in training for decades, this is obvious. For others, this is not so obvious. Our present situation gives us a glimpse into what is to come. How beneficial is that? We, over the last two years, have now had experience, at least indirectly, with riots, church burnings, flash looting, autonomous zones, understaffing due to defund the police efforts and many other things we have not had experience with previously. These and new areas will continue to rapidly surface in the near future.

Tested and True: What we veteran trainers know is that tactical training also shapes attitudes and beliefs. That sounds very strange, but this is a tested and true principle. Whether used in police or military training, we know that at the beginning of a basic training session, new officers come into the academy walking, talking, acting like civilians. We force them to begin to act like police officers in the way they dress, in their demeanor, in their language. We teach proper police skills which further pushes this indoctrination. New recruits march, use the words sir and ma'am, and are required to display discipline and focus in many ways. At the end of several months of this intense training, these new officers now walk, talk, and act like police officers. This transformative process actually works rather well. The military services of the world have known and used this for millennia.

How does this relate to ethics when giving advanced practical skills like riot training? Well, by showing and practicing what is acceptable and what is not, because of certain moves being overly brutal or immoral, one is actually also training professional ethics within these physical tactics. An 18-inch "riot" baton was commonly used in training in the 1970s. Jabs with this weapon to the chest area and arms were taught as proper, whereas jabs to the face, neck and groin, and strikes to the head were not proper. Can you see how we are actually teaching morals and police ethics in those tactical training exercises as well? As difficult as these situations will be tactically in the future, these will be even more difficult to handle psychologically and morally.

We cannot train in every potential situation an officer might face, tactically or morally, thus, we need to have these overarching principles so that they can address each of these new challenges using those principles. Unless officers have some understanding of the virtues, they are like a ship—adrift without a rudder or an anchor.

Without Training and Discussions, We Just Don't Know What to Do!

Doing the "Right" Thing: There were a couple of western sheriffs over the course of the last two years (2020 and 2021) who publicly said that their departments were not going to enforce certain decrees because they were unconstitutional. There were other departments that arrested people passing out literature—who were observing the distancing and masking requirements—outside of an abortion clinic, just as they had been doing for years under a court authorization. They were arrested at that time for a supposed no-gather decree violation for "non-essential activity" when these same people could walk down the street to a big-box store and gather with hundreds of people within an enclosed structure. Of course, we now know that alternative goals were actually a motivation for focusing on the anti-abortion groups and churches. We also now have experience—after the reversal of *Roe*—with how radical the abortion rights element in our society can become.

Police elsewhere wrote $500.00 tickets for everyone in a car, *including the children*, who were in a church parking lot listening to the pastor giving a sermon over the radio. Both the sheriffs and their deputies mentioned above and those police officers arresting anti-abortion groups probably had a gut feeling that they were doing "*the **right thing***." Wow! How wide a gap is that? There were hundreds of these types of incidents in 2020. Wouldn't it be nice to have some predetermined moral principles upon which to base a decision rather than just a snap "gut feeling" for these *1938 Moments*?

More Control – A Tighter Grip

As things become more chaotic, the natural human reaction is to become more controlling, more restrictive, more draconian without even acknowledging any contravening consideration like morality or justice or Constitutional principles. The "us against them" mindset that happens in some law enforcement circles is magnified in these times and in those situations. These issues will probably lead to substantial criticism for law enforcement in the future.

A Time-Tested Maxim: The granting of greater authority to the police could—almost certainly will—result in greater abuses by the police. Lord Anton, recognizing history [smart man], famously said, "***Power tends to corrupt and absolute power corrupts absolutely.***" History shows this happens over and over. Why should we expect our police officers to be any different? The rest of his quote—not often reported—is even more sobering. This is: "**Great men are almost always bad men …**" I would modify that somewhat by claiming, *Great men* (all policemen in such an era) *will likely* ***become*** *bad men when unchecked by* ***morals, rules,*** *or* ***self-discipline***!

When we ask: *How are these tactical things connected to officers becoming more professional and ethical*, we can see links, if we look closely, between virtue training and street encounters, riot training and decree enforcement, good discretion and Defund the Police movements. There are a few lesser noticed ramifications for bad policing as well.

The Catch-22 Provision: The failure to prepare for these things will also, I believe, have a massive negative impact in a surprising way that most administrators have not really contemplated. We will, of course, receive negative publicity from the media and special interest groups, as we always do during such times, but we will also experience the even more devasting impact of a *mass exodus* of officers from departments and the profession if we do not prepare officers for these times, and this will **largely be our own fault**! What will be the result?

Staffing – Are there ramifications when a two-year officer on a department is considered a veteran? Are there ramifications when shift sergeants only have three to four years of experience? Are there ramifications when a department is thirty percent understaffed? Do challenging situations, handled correctly, have the potential to push us over the top as being accepted as true professionals as well as have the potential to drive us back into the dark ages if these things are handled badly? Will the way we handle immoral decrees reflect on our professionalism?

We have been posing a critical question at the end of these last few chapters. The overarching question for our street officers when confronting these chaotic, explosive, 1938 Moment situations is: *Why should I employ any discipline or restraint whatsoever*? The answer: **Your personal moral code requires this**! ❖

Chapter 10

History as Our Schoolmaster

King Solomon Speaks Again

In this chapter, we harken back to King Solomon's pronouncement that history repeats itself. More specifically, Solomon said, ***that*** which was, is ***that*** which shall be. It seems that many things are now aligning in ways *very similar* to the way they aligned in 1967 in America and in the 1930s in Nazi Germany.

For this reason, we will take this important trip into the history of those days to see:

1) if things that are happening today generally match with what happened then (in the 1930s, especially), and if so,
2) if those events will be consequential end-times mile markers (worth monitoring) by comparing those events to Bible prophecy, and then,
3) if we can specifically anticipate if this or that might happen again *in our near future* because of the history-repeating-itself principle, and finally,
4) if we might change these seemingly absolute results for the better this time around.

As for this last point, we know we cannot change Bible prophecy—it always comes to pass—but we might be able to change it for some individuals. Because of free will, some may choose to come towards the light (if we give them the tools to discern what is actually occurring) rather than ending their days in darkness, like so many of the elite German commanders did.

Our theme for this chapter will, of course, be that history repeats itself. This is largely rooted in the axiom that human nature has not changed one lick over the ages. I know, I am beating this concept to death as well, but most are not so sure that "history really repeats itself" until they come to grips with human nature. We humans are predictably disreputable and untrustworthy! Only after accepting this reality, can we successfully progress through this chapter.

I also know, humans typically want more than this abstract proof of effectiveness. In our attempt to predict what is likely to be just around the corner, we also need to ask—for credibility purposes—if there are "foreshadows and types" that have already occurred and proved accurate. Not surprisingly, yes, there have been many such examples. Here are a few.

Partisan Enforcement

When we previously defined the term *justice*—an important concept for ethical police officers—one of the definitions mentioned that "partisan enforcement" is the *antithesis* of the justice concept. Considering the Gestapo's focus on the Jews and then the FBI's recent identification and prosecution of over 700 people participating in the January 6th riot, but then also considering the many riots, burnings, and attacks on the federal courthouse in Portland, disorders and burnings in Minneapolis and across the country for *more than one year* which received no such federal attention, there seems a strong repetition of history here. If history is a teacher, and it is, should we then prepare for increasingly partisan enforcement efforts, like the Gestapo conducted (considered part of the SS, the secret police) during the 1930s and like what might easily occur with a hugely expanded IRS criminal enforcement division (87,000 new agents) here in America? Seems likely. "**That**" which was is "**that**" which shall be.

Should local law enforcement officers maintain a high vigilance for partisan enforcement and publicly voice our professional concern over heavy prosecution of trivial violations for ***political purposes****?*

Consider the DOJ's refusal to enforce the federal law prohibiting demonstrators from picketing in front of (conservative) Supreme Court justices' homes. What about the lack of federal law enforcement responses to the burnings of pro-life facilities and churches after the *Roe* decision was reversed in 2022? Is this like the lack of response from the German police for the burnings in the Jewish business district in 1938? Do the Antifa and BLM groups match the tactics of Hitler's Youth Corps in the 1930s? If so, can we then predict what will likely be happening next concerning the crime of arson?

Are arrests of all such law violators—not just conservative rioters—critical to curb this chaos and these riots, burnings, and property destructions?

If history is any teacher [I know, you have heard this before], this abusive use of law enforcement seems to be *a favorite tactic* for tyrannical administrations.

Arson As a Modus Operandi (MO)
Calling Good Evil and Evil Good

Can we now anticipate what direction we are heading, using the Hitler youth corps model with our young people today? King Solomon seems to think so. Perhaps the burnings and attacks on churches and pro-life organizations in 2022 should not surprise us. Will there be more of this? Think of the religious persecutions in Germany in the

1930s. Remember also the "Reichstag Fire" burning of the German parliament building. Now check prophecy. Does it say Christians will be persecuted? Might we see the Left accuse conservatives and Christians of doing what they are doing? Might we see evil acts being called good (transgender facilitation efforts) and good (Christian religious practices) being called evil? That Solomon guy really knew his stuff!

So, should we in law enforcement be preparing for substantial persecution of religions in the near future, even in America? Might this happen through "hate" laws? What types of assaults will be happening? With history being a teacher, perhaps assaults and burnings will be two favorite tactics for anarchists. What does that mean for law enforcement? In the short run, perhaps we will need some immediate arson investigation training in our departments and a few new op-plans.

In Germany, only the Lutheran faith saw some tolerance. The entire faith of Judaism was pushed out of their society, with other faiths falling somewhere between the two of these. Judging from Germany, will we see a narrowing of allowed religions? If history is a teacher, we will see exactly that! We can probably expect to see religions narrowed down to one approved conglomerate religion with high persecution of others. Besides point #2, at the very beginning of this chapter (how does this compare to prophecy?), and point #3 (history repeats itself), such an observation reveals much. This is exactly what prophecy says will eventually happen, see Revelation 13. So, is there a ***high*** probability that religions will be narrowed and persecuted in the near future? Is there a high probability that religions will eventually meld into a one-world religion? Yes!

Christianity a Primary Target: Christianity will have its doctrines mixed with other dogmas. Those denominations that attempt to maintain their pure doctrines will be targeted and choked off. It will be interesting to see the direction that King Charles III, Great Britain's new monarch, will take. I used to think that Pope Francis was the most interesting person to watch in this ecumenical movement—in recent years making agreements with Islam and the Buddhists and previous fusions with liberal Protestants and the Lutherans—but now I am not sure. King Charles III is very supportive of Islam, but now (after his coronation as king) he is also the head of the Church of England. Interesting! This dynamic may bear watching. Likewise, there is going to be a massive synod at the Vatican in 2023 that could be a turning point. Stay tuned!

Should the police attempt to protect those religions or should we join in with the one-world religious push? You decide using your new set of ethical standards. If history is any teacher, orthodox and evangelical denominations will be *targeted first*, and *radical antisemitism* will again explode across the world. Eventually, the consolidated religion will support the political state and become the state authorized religion.

Local police should receive instruction in arson investigation, illegal threats and intimidations, and in radical anti-religious groups (worldviews).

Police should receive instruction on First Amendment limits on police conduct, especially conduct concerning religious practices, which includes tolerance for differing religious affiliations including Judaism, Islam, occultism, and atheism (BUT NOT for illegal activities within those religions).

What will likely happen after that is pretty easy to predict. Just look back to any political system in history where a "state religion" was established. Islam, Hinduism, and, yes, even Christianity has had some very bad moments. Were there actual religious wars during the Protestant Reformation? What happened in the Inquisition? How about the Crusades? What occurred in 1492 in Spain? What happened in England when King Edward took over as head of the church? That part of our future predictions is pretty easy, even without checking the prophecies.

We mentioned that 2020 came upon law enforcement as a total surprise. Draconian decrees, overreaches, and Constitutional violations were the norm for more than a year. If history is a teacher [Got it! Find a new phrase], we now recognize how our elected officials will act when this fear scenario is repeated. We are no longer ignorant on these things, friend. Should we prepare for that day?

Are intradepartmental discussions, perhaps even roundtables, important for preparing officers for these overreactions in the future?

We know that Nero and the Nazis (the Reichstag Fire) both blamed their opposition for doing what they actually did in order to justify some pretty despicable retaliations. Will this tactic likely continue in this age?

Will the radical Left increasingly use claims of non-inclusiveness, discrimination, and hate to subjugate (discriminate against) conservatives, Republicans, truthful news reporters, the Supreme Court, Christians and Christian churches? Should we in law enforcement guard against falling into these deceptions and protect those vulnerable groups?

Was all of this deduced by using King Solomon's mantra? Well, yes: Solomon's mantra, history, current events, and the Bible.

You, Too, Can *and Should* Use This Technique!

These few demonstrations of the first step in how to prepare for the future are examples of how administrators, and officers for that matter, can use what has occurred to accurately predict what will be. There are hundreds of areas like the above examples in which we could use this technique to generally "predict" future trends—not prophesy specific events—but trends, even unusual trends. Solomon seemed to know what he was talking about. Remember, human nature has not changed even if those secular humanists claim that it has, or they claim—even more preposterously—that we are much more sophisticated now than we were in the 1930s.

We will identify several more important such areas (below) and dig a little deeper into some to show what is coming. These new areas, however, are not directly related to things for which law enforcement can directly prepare or control, but they are presented here so that law enforcement can anticipate, i.e., know where we are on the timeline. You will also see that these examples lead us into a *very important* area of consideration for law enforcement. That area is ***inspiring leadership*** through having heroes and mentors.

Other Failures in 1938 – The Church (this is an important one as well): Why didn't pastors and the churches take a stand in Germany? Mostly for the same reasons that law enforcement did not. There are many stories, anecdotal evidence, perhaps only legends, about the trains heading to Auschwitz, passing by churches. The church congregants would sing louder as the trains passed by to drown out the screams of the Jews emanating from the boxcars.

The churches of that day felt like they were in a very tenuous position, and they should therefore keep a very low-profile. This seems like the anthesis of what churches are called to do, but it was a fact of the times, and people were scared. Does this give us a "prediction" on how most churches will be acting in the next couple of years? [Wow, perhaps we are becoming prophets. Not really.]

Apostasy: Officers may have heard of the one-world government and the one-world religion, Revelation 13. The prophecy on this says that churches will stray further and further away from traditional (biblical) values in the latter-days, a process called apostasy. That seems a good guess for what is happening right now (see news stories on denominational splits). Using our "predictive" protocol and what happened in Germany during those stressful days that looks very much like our condition today, what should we expect to happen in the near future concerning apostasy, especially when combining the biblical prophecy on apostasy with the biblical prophecy having to do with birth pangs?

That can give us a really good guess on our timeline. Keep attuned to this, and you will know where we are concerning the Great Reset. We might expect that traditional dogmas (core church teachings) will be radically changing in the very near future.

Test This Yourself – Believe it or not, you can actually test this claim. Ask your pastor if your church provides classes on end-time biblical prophecy. This would, of course, confirm to the congregation what is likely to happen *with their church* in the very near future! Because of this—the likely answer to your prophecy question in almost every church—is that they do not teach this because it is hard to understand, it is only allegorical, it scares the congregants, or all prophecy was fulfilled by AD 70 (not so). That one-quarter to one-third of the Bible (prophecy) is just ignored today.

This is, of course, understandable (but not excusable) as most churches are under pressure because church numbers are waning and outside influences are becoming increasingly hostile towards religion, especially the Christian and Jewish religions, to the point that some churches have been recently desecrated and/or firebombed, supposedly because of the 2022 *Roe* reversal decision, and everybody is just a little scared.

A good question to ask your pastor: Why didn't they (the churches) immediately file suit in county court to enjoin mayors, the governor, and health department officers from classifying churches as non-essential or to stop those officials from outright closing their churches when thousands of businesses were not closed during those two years? After all, the practice of a religion is a *Constitutional right*. In fact, it is the first right mentioned in the First Amendment. Is the right to open a liquor store in the Constitution?

Another good question: Did your church reopen with a more "woke" philosophy after the pandemic? If so, ask why. Perhaps officers should ask their pastors what the Bible requires of the church in times of moral decay and corruption. Is it to hide in the church basement. [Perhaps a little too snarky.]

If it sounds as if I am coming down pretty hard on pastors, I am. The church and pastors are hugely influential in a community. They have been the force that, in the past, has driven communities in a certain noble direction.

Many pastors today say that they should not be involved in politics. Churches do not need to support specific candidates, but they should support biblical issues and philosophies and those who hold those beliefs. Just hiding in our churches seems so counterproductive. For a good case study on this, notice how involved pastors were during our American Revolution and the Great Awakening in our country's formative years. Notice how many pastors were involved in writing our founding documents. Research if there was a religious element in the community established by the Mayflower Compact or if the concept of "inalienable rights" has a religious component to it. If pastors did not provide moral foundations and teachings in those days, we almost certainly would not have a United States today.

Should the church strive to get society to conform to biblical standards or should churches strive to conform to current cultural standards? What does Jesus say on this?

The history of the Nazi party sounds very much like an operator's manual for overthrowing a culture or governmental system or perhaps even the entire world. Does that sound like what is happening today? Speaking of "sounding like," close your eyes and *listen* to Klaus Schwab present some of his ideas. Sorry, I digress. Nevertheless, if you take the time to notice, you will find that very few of our churches today preach the tough biblical messages. We have largely lost these institutions as moral examples for our citizens.

Do not despair, however. **History** shows us a few great examples. Mentors, even if long gone, have always been very influential, e.g.,

Abraham Lincoln, Teddy Roosevelt, Dr. Martin Luther King. They give purpose, direction and power to movements and courage to citizens. This last statement provides a hint, perhaps even a Sherlock Holmes-type clue for our police services ["a clue for our police services" get it; yah, I know, snarky again]. The Left has been astoundingly well funded, organized, and dedicated—in a very loud and obnoxious way—since 2020. I was one of many who was shocked by how fast and comprehensively the Left moved in March of 2020 and thereafter. They obviously have been planning these things for years. Notice the Forum of Young Global Leaders, from about 1992. I am impressed by the way they never give up. Why are conservatives afraid to come out and take a stand? Maybe this next section will help.

Mentors and Heroes

For new police officers, mentors can be a very strong role models, even if they have passed on. Using examples of noble people, their quotations and life deeds, like our Founding Fathers, etc., are powerful. We have not tapped into this in any substantial way in recent years. Perhaps we should use this technique again.

Since this chapter is about history, I will present two inspiring examples from those days of Nazism that are highly relevant for today. Use these examples for yourself and relate these to others, many others! Both are powerful! The first is the story of Pastor Deitrick Bonhoeffer. He was a pastor who did not cower.

The Deitrick Bonhoeffer Story

Bonhoeffer was a Lutheran pastor in the 1930s when Hitler was coming to power. He spent some time in America where he began attending a black (African-American) church in Harlem, New York, during those days of strict segregation. It was that experience that showed him how to survive and administer a church in a hostile environment. He saw what was happening in his homeland at that time and returned to Germany to become a pastor there. Upon his return, he began speaking out about the Nazis and Hitler.

He helped lead a resistance movement against Hitler's regime, almost from Hitler's ascent to power in 1933. Consequently, he was harassed by the Nazis for years, prohibited from speaking in public, and required to regularly report ***to the police*** to document all his activities. He was also involved in a schism in his church denomination when the Nazis came to power. Sound familiar? Think: the Methodists!

He was active in the underground resistance movement during that time and evaded Hitler's Gestapo through those years and most of the war years until 1943 when he was finally arrested. While detained in a concentration camp in 1945, he was accused of participating in a conspiracy to assassinate Adolf Hitler. Most have heard of that unsuccessful assassination attempt. He was quickly tried and convicted and hanged at that concentration camp on April 9, 1945. Here is the irony. What an irony! Germany gave its unconditional surrender on May 7, 1945, less than one month after Bonhoeffer was hanged. For a good overview of Bonhoeffer during this time, read the book, ***Seven Men: And the Secret to Their Greatness***, by Eric Metaxas.

Ironically, if he could have survived for one more month, he would have undoubtedly been declared a living hero and would have had an extremely bright future in politics or religion or business. His dedication to resisting Hitler over many years *was a real oddity* within the German religious community in those years.

Why didn't he go the way of so many other pastors of that day—and police officers—by just going with the flow? It was probably his strong moral underpinning, masterfully revealed in the *Seven Men* book. **Do you see where I am going?** This is a great lesson for us today. Although involving an entirely different discussion, too lengthy for this book, I also believe our educational system over the last two decades has perpetuated the strong likelihood of such atrocities occurring again today (remember the Hitler youth corps).

Nancy Wake, A Superhero

Another person who stands out during this time of trouble is Nancy Wake. Wake became part of the French Resistance in World War II, performing espionage missions against the Nazis, blowing up bridges, and successfully accomplishing many other dangerous exploits. She was fearless and tough as nails. She was beaten and was nearly captured several times. She once rode 200 km (about 125 miles) each way on a bicycle to complete a mission. Her real talent, though, was that she had the uncanny ability to read and manipulate people and to get through all sorts of Nazi checkpoints. It was not long before she was placed on Germany's most-wanted list. They labeled her the "White Mouse."

Wake did not have to do any of this. She was a journalist and the wife of a rich merchant and could have lived a luxurious life in either England or the United States. Her full, rather astounding, story can be found through researching her name on the Internet. She was highly decorated in five countries after the war, became part of the new fledgling intelligence community just forming in those days, and lived to the age of 88 (dying in 2011). There is also a very interesting documentary video made of her exploits which you can view on YouTube and Amazon Prime, titled: *Nancy Wake: Gestapo's Most Wanted*. She was truly a superhero's superhero!

Should each of us adopt a hero, who we can publicly recommend and proclaim to others, who will also give us a model to admire and follow?

The Other End of the Spectrum – Rudolf Hess, the Anti-superhero: Think: Nuremberg Trials. Hess was held in Spandau Prison (dedicated to confine German "war criminals") until 1987 when he allegedly committed suicide. One of my deputies, before his civilian police employment, was on the Army security force that guarded Hess at Spandau Prison. Surprisingly, Hess actually made a secret solo flight to Scotland in 1941 to propose a peace treaty. Nonetheless, he was convicted as a war criminal years later.

Three points here. Point #1: Hess never got out of a cell from 1941 through 1987 (46 years) because he committed many crimes against humanity in the early days of the Nazi party. Point #2: There is very little forgiveness for these types of crimes, even years later. He did not get to associate with other prisoners during any of that time and was, in fact, the only prisoner left in that prison by 1987. Point #3: All of this happened, including his atrocities, within a couple of generations of today. This *is not* ancient history! If conditions that manifested in Germany in those days largely mirror the conditions manifesting in the world today, might a substantial number of police officers have a ***1938 Moment*** in the not-too-distant future ***and choose wrongly?*** Once deciding to go with the flow, officers can be sucked down into *a deep cesspool* very quickly!

For those officers who consider going with the flow, it is instructive to remember that besides there being little forgiveness, such crimes against humanity *are not quickly forgotten, either*. The Mossad (the Israeli intelligence agency) hunted down war criminals all over the world for decades after that country came back into existence in 1948.

The Judeo-Christian worldview, discussed in Chapter 12, is really beneficial for officers in this regard in that those who accept this worldview believe they will stand before God someday to give an account of their actions while on earth. This belief, ***by itself***, instills a sense of restraint in most and is a much better mindset than to think everybody will just forgive and forget a few years after such atrocities happen. Case in point, here is a ***very** recent*, sobering news headline:

> "101-year-old former Nazi concentration camp guard sentenced to five years for Holocaust atrocities," CNN, 6/28/**2022** [pay particular attention to the date].

Do we, in the police services, learn from history and prepare for the future, or do we just continually get caught unprepared and off guard?

There May Be No Assurance of Stability in the Constitution or in Our Country in Years to Come

History teaches that every country has an end. The above title comes from this realization and a study of history. We often have a false sense of security thinking we are protected by our Constitution and our individual Constitutional rights, but these are perhaps a little more delicate than what one might think. As mentioned previously, if fewer and fewer people care about these rights, does it matter what the Constitution actually says if the Constitution is just ignored by our leaders? We are getting a taste of this already!

We mentioned how powerful stories and quotations from our Founding Fathers can be for enhancing patriotism and bravery. Here are a few such quotations from our Founding Fathers concerning their beliefs on the robustness of our Constitution. Do these quotations give some insight on how they felt about the durability of our Constitution?

Quotations From Our Founding Fathers

Here a few quotations from our Founding Fathers having to do with the frailty of our Constitution:

> John Adams famously said, "Our Constitution was made only for a moral and religious people. It is wholly inadequate to the government of any other."
>
> Samuel Adams said, "While the people are virtuous, they cannot be subdued, but when they lose their virtue, then will be ready to surrender their liberties to the first external or ***internal*** [author's emphasis added] invader."
>
> Daniel Webster said, "To preserve the government, we must also preserve morals."
>
> Benjamin Franklin said, "Only a virtuous people are capable of freedom." On another occasion, after being asked what kind of government have you designed for us, he replied, "A republic, if you can keep it."
>
> Benjamin Rush (our first surgeon general) said, "Without virtue there can be no liberty."
>
> Thomas Jefferson was very suspicious of the Supreme Court, even in those days, as not being up to the task of preserving liberties or good Constitutional interpretations. He once said about John Marshall's opinion on the *Marbury* case, "... twistifications in the case of Marbury ... shew [show] how dexterously he can reconcile law to his personal biases ..." Can using politics rather than Constitutional principles for deciding a case, e.g., *Roe v.*

> *Wade* (1973), result in many decades (almost fifty years) of civil strife and conflict within a nation?

A little book like this could be filled with quotations from our Founding Fathers on the questionable durability of our Constitution and country, but it is evident from these few quotations that our Founding Fathers thought our system would crumble when virtue is lost, even with a remaining military.

Patriotism

If the majority of our citizens do not believe in the provisions within our Constitution, they are null and void even though this document continues to be prominently displayed at our National Archives building. So, is virtue even more important for our country's police officers, who are really our governmental leaders on the sidewalks of our nation, than for the average citizen? You be the judge.

Recommendation: Concerning the overarching question for this chapter: Can we lessen the impact of these undesirable situations on our communities and on our officers using the professionalization process? Yes, I absolutely believe so!

The parts of our professionalization process having to do with ethics, virtue, and character have a potential for providing somewhat of a shield and buffer for our citizens ***and*** for our officers through instilling some moral foundations and establishing some ethical armor—canons of conduct—within the departments.

These standards give a *reason to act honorably*. Police administrators and training officers will need to be the initial spark to start the process. Once geared to thinking in this manner, however, even line officers will undoubtedly be able to find a number of areas in which a moral belief can and should be ***enshrined*** into a professional standard.

I realize that our examination of the Nazis in the pre-war period may have been a little tedious for a book on police ethics, but I think it very instructive. Most of the pre-World War II events show how a society and country can be reshaped surprisingly quickly. If history is a teacher [do you now think it is?], just ignoring or twisting the Constitution seems highly likely in the future [another sage prophetic observation].

I suspect that President Biden has already set an all-time record for having his executive orders declared unconstitutional by the courts, including the Supreme Court. Is that a record to be proud of? It is not surprising to this author that he continues to malign the SCOTUS. Modern man has certainly not developed or progressed past the point of moral turpitude, i.e., human nature, when the conditions are right. Will this be the case in the future?

We now have the tools so that we can anticipate what to expect in the near future with a little contemplation. Every officer and administrator can now use this technique to prepare for a hundred and one challenging areas. The final question for this chapter is: Will our officers and administrators make the right choice and be able to perform nobly at their 1938 Moment? ❖

Chapter 11

Worldviews: The Good, the Bad, and the Ugly

We will attempt somewhat of a sales pitch here, as we have in previous chapters. In this chapter, it may seem as if we have drifted far away from our theme of police ethics and police professionalism into a discussion on world ethics having nothing to do with law enforcement, but we have not. First of all, this subject of worldviews is much more important today for police officers than it has ever been. Knowing how splinter groups think in this fractious world today is important. Knowing what our best outlook (perspective) probably should be for enduring the slings and arrows to come is also worthwhile.

In our last several chapters, we presented some likely future events to make the completion of an officer's day-to-day duties a little easier. The subject of worldviews fits nicely into this structure. A worldview is really a congealing of a number of virtues or attributes into a philosophy (an ethos) which is really a group-think *that actually materializes in our society*. Why certain attributes congeal into forming a worldview is much too complex of a subject for this little book. We will just recognize that they do and report on a few of these worldviews with which officers regularly interact or will likely interact in the future.

A study of a few worldviews not only shows some virtuous attributes that people have identified over the ages—that an officer probably should consider adopting—but also alerts officers to dangerous groups and what they might do in the future. Studying these worldviews is somewhat like studying criminal personality profiles. Of course, not all worldviews entice criminal activity, but some do, and knowing about these, mostly occultic, worldviews is worthwhile.

Likewise, we are not trying to sell *a worldview* as the one that all officers must follow although you will undoubtedly notice my enthusiasm for the Judeo-Christian ethic. Is it true that certain worldviews help create a better officer? I think so, but we will look at a few of these and let you decide.

Like other subjects discussed previously in this book, this area is very easily expanded into in-service training topics. Our examination of this subject cannot be comprehensive or this work would not be *The* ***Little*** *Blue Book on Police Ethics*. Nonetheless, the few examples we will provide here are more than enough to start a good conversation. So, let us take a brief look at seven worldviews that have some elements that bear upon police professionalism or law enforcement, including the bad and ugly ones, and there are a number of those.

Seven Illustrative Worldviews

We begin this examination with one secular view that has very few useful elements for law enforcement—hedonism—but it is worthwhile for comparisons and provides a ground-zero starting point. After next examining several more beneficial worldviews, we will conclude with several religiously-based worldviews including the occultic worldviews, and yes, these are religious worldviews. And finally, we will present a brief description of the Judeo-Christian worldview to help introduce our next chapter. But to get us started, let us look at what the hedonists say.

Hedonism

We will start from near the bottom, as I rate these worldviews for their desirability for law enforcement. Hedonism is the most selfish and prideful of the views presented here. This is the *if it feels good, do it* philosophy that has gripped our culture for the past fifty years. It is self-centered and disregards other views, conditions, and situations unless those other views or situations help one to ultimately help oneself. This is what was famously professed, month after month, in *Playboy Magazine* when it was, in the 1960s and 1970s, still a giant in the publication world. According to that publication, sexual norms of the day and abstinence were to be shunned.

Selfless acts and service to others are not really relevant in this worldview. Life is meant to be lived to the fullest. Materialism, a primary idol in our society during the last four to five decades, is good according to this viewpoint. A big house, flashy cars, big boats, large motorcycles, and a number of expensive electronic devices are all part of the mindset. He who dies with the most toys wins! As we move into the extremes of this mindset today, we (as a society) are just now beginning to realize that this worldview does nothing to fill that unexplainable void in us. Thus, it has today lost some of its attractiveness as a primary view.

Hedonism provides a good starting point for this discussion as it has been so accepted over the past several decades. This worldview provides very few beneficial attributes for law enforcement other than when officers are negotiating for better conditions and higher wages or for training for self-preservation. We will next examine a traditional worldview that has been in mainstream thought for centuries.

Utilitarianism

This is an interesting worldview that has been used by some of our heroes. It is a thinking process in which we weigh good and bad on the scale of eventual-outcomes, perhaps even very distant outcomes. It can also be an *end justifies the means* thought-process. I cite this worldview as one of the first in our mainstream views as this thought process used to be very common, but now has also been eclipsed by more "trendy" worldviews (discussed below) which are not just amoral (like hedonism) but aggressively anti-God. Unlike hedonism, the utilitarianism philosophy actually takes detailed, careful looks at the competing interests and how they affect others. The ultimate decision on what to do rests on what alternative will produce *the greatest good for the greatest number of people.*

This sounds really noble on first impression, but can be anything but noble or moral under certain conditions. A utilitarian view can "justify" devastating slaughters of large numbers of people if the final outcome will "improve" the world, i.e., the greater good. General George Patton, one of our American heroes, knew from his military intelligence command and experience that more than 10,000 soldiers would likely lose their lives in the Battle of the Bulge, but he still gave the order as the alternative would be to allow German forces to break through the lines, regroup, and possibly surround the Allied Forces.

We Americans viewed this battle as sealing our victory on the western front during World War II but this single battle actually cost 19,000 American lives and 89.000 American casualties. The brutally cold weather was as much of an enemy as were the German forces. My father was part of this battle and returned home with both some minor shrapnel wounds and trench foot. This is a pretty stark example of the *end justifies the means* thought process.

This worldview can be nefariously used for supporting just about anything for a *promised* "good" conclusion. Some devastating examples were the communist takeovers in Russia, China and other Eastern European countries, and more recently, in Venezuela. Venezuela was, in fact, one of the richest countries in the world but is now nearly destitute after the socialist takeover.

A modern-day, real-world example of the misuse of this philosophy is the "Great Reset" campaign being presently pushed by the World

Economic Forum (WEF). The claims made by the WEF are very attractive. "You will own nothing and be happy." The WEF, by its own admission, is using fear and the coronavirus to complete these schemes. Their goal is a socialistic one-world government, and they are much closer to implementing this than most U.S. citizens realize. So, while a utilitarian mindset can produce a truly beneficial result for mankind, it can also have some very devastating and demonic results.

The obvious problem with this view is when the noble outcome is not achieved, either through actual failure or preplanned (schemed) failure. In such a situation, you have subjected many to some very devastating things while progressing towards this "promised" outcome. All of those sacrifices (the "means") were for naught because the "outcome" was devastating as well. In the case of General George Patton, the campaign waged in the Battle of the Bulge was the correct decision, at least for us Americans. It did not, however, work out so well for the Germans.

As a viewpoint for our modern American police officer, we often need to think along the lines of "the greatest good" for a particular situation or for our communities—a very noble approach—but we must also consider if "the means" are noble or at least moral, in addition to the hoped-for outcomes. Is roughing up a suspect to teach him a lesson after he has pushed an older lady to the ground to snatch her purse justified under this worldview?

Ethical Naturalism

Ethical Naturalism claims that we can study the "natural sciences" for insights into morality. It claims that inquiry into the natural world (science) can increase our moral knowledge, and it largely professes that science is a foundation upon which moral decisions can be based. This field of study has looser boundaries than most other ethical disciplines, and this thought process veers into areas like evolution as well as moral relativism. This philosophy uses evidence from biology, primatology (the study of primates, monkeys), psychology, and neurology to classify and explain moral/immoral behavior. This, like many *of **man's created** philosophies*, has some problems.

Suppose we say killing each other is bad. This generally conforms to our scientific reasoning (naturalism) as we know that the repeated large-scale slaughtering of our species will eventually result in a trigger point that would likely cause the extinction of mankind. But what if, as an example, there were people who had developed an immunity to a highly deadly virus, but we could not harvest enough of this "immunity" factor from their tissues to save mankind unless we killed all of these immunity carriers to obtain every milligram of immunity serum? Here is your moralistic justification (and perhaps even a utilitarian justification) stated as a "scientifically" determined fact. Are we now justified in the killing of that group to save mankind as a whole? We absolutely know, through science, that harvesting that amount of immunity serum from that group will supply just enough to save mankind.

This "scientific" thought process has been embraced by many today. "**Follow the science**" is a mantra we hear over and over again today. The trouble is that it has no absolutes. It can be used to come to whatever conclusion one wants. It falls right into the maxim: Figures don't lie, but liars can figure!

I foresee this as a way to justify euthanasia in the future if it is scientifically determined, for instance, that someone has lost 97% or more of his usefulness to society because of his advanced old age compared to the expense of supporting him. Margaret Sanger, founder of what became Planned Parenthood, was an unapologetic advocate of reducing the number of people from certain races within society to make the society stronger and healthier. This mindset would also justify "euthanasia committees," as claimed would eventually happen during the arguments on the Obama health care program. Could this rationale limit the time a person can be on a respirator or in intensive care?

For officers and police administrators, this "scientific" thought process can often be used to sell a program to a secular city council because ***the science*** supports this! It can, unfortunately, also be used for filling internment camps or for the never-ending erosion of our First Amendment rights or for confiscating guns, or for giving police officers unchecked street authority or for many other abuses of our citizens. Should we always, "Follow the science"? Here is something for you to consider: Doesn't *every* new scientific find replace an older scientific find that we thought was scientifically sound, perhaps even anointed at the time, only to find that it now needs discarding? Have we ever witnessed the misuse *of science* to justify some irrational and rather draconian restrictions or abuses?

Secular Humanism

Secular humanism is a philosophy of life that embraces human "reason" rather than divine direction, or even science. It is a *very* popular worldview today. It claims man can determine what is moral, right or wrong, by just thinking about the alternatives. We do not even need science here to validate our conclusions. If some of us decide, after thinking about it, that there is no reason we should not have three or four sexual partners at a time, it must be alright, at least for me. After all, we are not hurting anyone. If someone else thinks it is alright to steal in order to have a better life, well that must be alright as well. Aiming for a better life is certainly admirable. After all, a victim generally has insurance.

Man is the Answer to Everything: This worldview specifically rejects religious dogma and supernaturalism. One can comfortably be a secular humanist if one is also an atheist or agnostic. This worldview does not claim that humans are inherently good or inherently bad, nor does it claim that humans are superior to nature or animals, thus "climate change" and "animal rights" ethics. The secular humanism philosophy overlaps several other philosophies like naturalism, evolutionism, and utilitarianism to some degree. This worldview seems, to this author, to be primarily a battle against God.

Technology vs. Human Nature: It claims that man can solve all of his own problems through reasoning to arrive at a utopian world without divine inspiration. In short, given enough time and thought, man can create a near-perfect world without war, starvation, or inequality. People see how we have advanced technologically over the years and think this is something that can actually be accomplished morally as well. Nevertheless, once a closer examination is made of our common character flaws, i.e., our human nature, it becomes apparent to most that we had a Hitler two generations ago, a Nero two millennia ago, a Nimrod before that and a Cain even before that, with many despots in between. After six thousand years of recorded history, it seems as if we should have gotten a lot closer to a utopian world than we are today.

The advancements in technology seem to really just give new despots the ability to be more efficient in their slaughters. Most of us view ourselves as pretty good, morally, although not many people claim to be perfect, which is the status required to enter heaven. Well, **if** we are not perfect, isn't this *really* saying that each of us really has a sin nature? If we have a sin nature, will we ever be successful at creating a utopian society, or will we be unintentionally successful at creating a gullible society?

There is a story, perhaps a myth, about the Indiana medical doctor who designed the Gatling Gun during the Civil War. This story claims that this doctor invented the gun because it was so devastating that everyone would be afraid to initiate any future wars after its production. That thought process certainly did not prove out.

I would suggest that this invention eventually also led to the 20mm electric motor-driven, six-barrel cannons mounted in helicopters during the Vietnam era and on fighter jets today (a truly devastating weapon) as well as all of the machineguns developed in those interceding years. The doctor's theory was what we call the "mutual deterrence" concept, more recently espoused for our nuclear weapons buildup during the Cold War. Even the nuclear "mutual deterrence" principle seems to be losing its credibility today. Unfortunately, there is an end-time Bible prophecy that sounds very much like a nuclear war, read Zechariah 14:12. Scary!

This "social evolution" belief is often used to sell Marxism, communism, and socialism today. If we use history as our guide, law enforcement will likely be seeing much more of this mindset in the coming years as justification for many morally corrupt endeavors like anti-vaxxer and re-education camps. Secular humanism is probably the dominant ethic in America today. For law enforcement, using logic and reason are good things. The problem is that this ethic can have many faulty reasoning processes that lead to very poor conclusions, like the Gatling Gun thought process.

Law enforcement will undoubtedly be called upon to enforce these corrupt ideas and efforts. After all, *any* "reasonable" person, no matter their personal medical history, should want a vaccination against COVID, and if they will not voluntarily take it, well ... you get the idea. Reason does not equal morality. Many philosophers have said for millennia that *reasonable people* can differ on certain issues. But doesn't that statement say that there is no standard? If you have one hundred people who differ slightly on an issue, who is right and what is moral? We kind of come back to the *what is truth* question that we examined early on in this text. The "truth question" is the real Achilles' heel of the Secular Humanist philosophy.

New Age Believers, Occultists, Wiccans, Wizards, Pagans, and Practitioners of Other Supernatural Worldviews

These religious views seem like a strange group to include in a set of worldviews that may strongly impact law enforcement and law enforcement professionalism in the future, but they are not! Likewise, it seems strange to some to classify these as "religious" systems. Why would law enforcement even be interested in such things? Well, I will put on my tinfoil hat and see if I can make sense of this for you.

What I will generally call occultic systems are, in fact, "deity" belief and worship systems. They are religious in the sense that they worship a supernatural being—usually meaning Satan or other fallen angels, although other names are often given to them—and are strongly anti-God (Jehovah) in nature. The term *pagan rituals* may seem more appropriate to some for what we will be addressing. I recently read a claim that the Wiccans recruited more new "believers" in 2019 than the Presbyterian Church. Wow! That is scary and sad!

Out of the Closet: Formerly, all of these occultic groups were mostly "in the closet," that is, until just the last few years. They now proudly occupy a large area of our public square. Pagan displays are everywhere. The Arch of Baal (Satan) was on tour just before the pandemic and was in New York City in 2016 and Washington D.C. in 2018. The term "New Age" is just another name for ancient occultic practices wrapped with flashy ribbon and a new bow.

One Common Denominator: I present these many groups in one subsection of this chapter because, when reduced to their common denominator, they are basically satanic, even though some do not claim this connection. Because of this satanic connection, I believe these worldviews to be more troublesome and dangerous than the previously discussed worldviews that may have a few good attributes for law enforcement, e.g., the greatest good for the greatest number, the *honest* use of science, and *non-delusional* reasoning. The satanic systems go to the very core of good vs. evil. These are worth our study via in-service training sessions.

We have already seen a few of these occultic groups claim to be "true religions" so that they can get the benefit of the First Amendment religious freedom protections. These will only become more prevalent and probably in-your-face in the future. Likewise, the Luciferians, the Illuminati, and the Freemasons hid their beliefs in a shroud of secrecy over the centuries. Today, however, just look at some of the artwork at the Denver Airport or at the E.U. building in Brussels (notice a statue of Europa and Zeus, the bull) to see how open this has become.

We have all heard of the pagan temples and religious practices of ancient Rome and Greece. Those demigods are what frame the pagan belief system that parallels the biblical account of fallen angels (Genesis 6:1-4), mighty men, men of renown, and giants (the old gods like Hercules, Zeus, and Thor). These are today framing our view of noble superheroes. Most young people do not realize that they were anything but noble and were a major reason for God causing the flood. We are being conditioned today to accept crossbred humans and genetic upgrades to mankind by these superhero movies and TV depictions. Why do I think this alarming? Because these belief systems afford humankind no beneficial value other than entertainment. More than the obvious problem of altering (corrupting) the human DNA (what could possibly go wrong there?), they rob society of a common foundation and recognizable standards. They further lead to division and chaos!

On the spiritual level, it is believed that as we corrupt the human genome, we get to a point that God will no longer allow us into heaven after death or protect us because we are no longer made in "His image." We (they) are someone else's creation. This has many ramifications that we do not have space to discuss here other than to say that adoption of occultic philosophies and practices leads to things radically different than what we would recognize or know today.

The public practice of occultic rituals ebbs and flows and is more or less visible or not depending on trends in society at the time. Many would be surprised at the number of followers in these pagan organizations, even within our national leaders. The practices of occultic groups can be traced back to well before the Roman Empire. Research: sacrifices to Moloch.

Truly Evil Practices: My point for this somewhat detailed discussion on occultic worldviews is that unlike many of the above contrived modern worldviews—meaning man-made—these occultic influences are more than just a product of modern man's creative mind. They really reflect the deep struggle from day one between good and evil. We fight not against flesh and blood, but against principalities, against powers, against the rulers of the darkness (satanic influences, Ephesians 6:12).

Even the Bible confirms that these entities—Apollo, for instance—will return at the darkest moment of our tribulation, Revelation 9:11. I will not attempt to convince even one of my readers that evil spirits are real. I will use my well-worn excuse that I have not the room in this ***Little Book*** of ethics to accomplish this. Nonetheless, even using just an historical perspective, it seems reasonable to anticipate that these occultic practices will continue to become more prevalent and accepted in our society.

Knowing that these worldviews will continue to surface, shouldn't we train on these?

If you are one who thinks these groups do not truly have any real impact on society, do a quick study of Adolph Hitler, his top command, and his secret police. They were all heavily involved in occultic practices. Our police should not be.

Many years ago while working the road, I was called by a farmer to a remote barn that had a large pentagram painted on the floor. At the time, I had no training or experience in those things and dismissed this incident as being merely a juvenile vandalism. Other officers related similar calls to me. I suspect that we completely missed what was truly going on at those sites.

Deception is Another Common Denominator: These groups will attempt to sell themselves as "good" influencers today by using terms like "White Witches" or "Christian Yoga." Occultic (satanic) organizations have many strategies, but the most common strategy *is **deception***. Yoga, very popular in America today, is actually a Hindu worship ritual.

This practice is often labeled as Christian Yoga, but this label does not change that it is a routine of physical movements that are designed as a worship ceremony to pagan (satanic) entities. If this is really innocent, why is this termed "Yoga" today rather than just stretching or flexibility training?

Worldviews that are based on demonic rituals—and forbidden to man in the Bible, meaning conjuring the spirits—have elements that are as seemingly innocuous as Yoga, Tarot Cards or Ouija Boards but are specifically designed to summon spirits (just as yelling down a hallway to someone does) and are meant to open portals. Those ceremonies and rituals open practitioners to more and deeper corruptions the longer they are practiced. Is this just because of normalizing that practice or is there something more at play here? Most people today, including Christians, do not believe that evil spirits can be conjured or that they even exist for that matter. Nonetheless, if people believe that prayer can pierce the dimensional barrier to reach the patriarchs, saints, dead relatives, Mother Mary, Jesus or God, why couldn't that also work to pierce the barrier to get to satanic spirits as well?

Occultic Views Generally: This discussion on occultic views has been a little more detailed than the other worldviews presented here, but these occultic views naturally lead to fracturing established religions and more chaos. If superheroes in our movies derive their powers from supernatural forces, aren't we being conditioned to believe wiccans or wizards can also pierce that veil to afford us those "desirable" attributes?

All I am asking you to do now is file these descriptions in the back of your brain. They may be worthwhile in the years to come. Or, you can, of course, disregard all of this. After all, everyone lives happily ever after in the superhero movies. Okay, I will hang up my tin hat now.

A Real Danger: Although most of the pagan beliefs are not a direct threat to law enforcement at this time, that may change in the very near future. There is a growing and powerful ecumenical movement in the world today to merge many religions. On the surface, this sounds really good. Can't everybody just get along? However, this ecumenical movement could, by design, easily morph into the one-world religion with the False Prophet, see Revelation 13.

Beyond the biblical warnings, ***history teaches*** that when a single religion also becomes a dominate (sovereign) political entity, bad things happen. Remember our mentioning Nero, the Crusades, the Inquisition, the Jewish Purge of 1492, as well as those we did not mention: King Henry, Bloody Mary, and especially Sharia Law!

Sharia Law: Ah, Sharia Law, there is a new one for American law enforcement, although this is not truly new to America. Our very first war after the Revolution was when Thomas Jefferson was President. He declared war on the Islamic pirates of the Barbary Coast. We are now, however, dealing with Islam internally. When I say most of these worldviews are not yet a direct threat to law enforcement, the one that will likely be the first real threat in America is Sharia Law.

Islam and Sharia Law

Sharia Law is of particular interest to us in law enforcement today because, in the short run, it is already taking over parts of America and supplanting Constitutional provisions and local law. This problem is considerably more extreme in Europe and Great Britain. There are parts of large cities in Europe and Great Britain that have been completely taken over by Sharia Law (Islam), research: 55 No-Go Zones in Sweden. You will likely be surprised by what you find when looking into this topic. Can we be far behind?

Insertion of Sharia Law is an excision of American sovereignty from within the United States, using small steps, inch by inch. How do we counter this?

This is particularly important in areas where Sharia Law is starting to manifest strongly. Sharia Law is an outgrowth of Islam. On the one hand, we need to respect all religious worship, our First Amendment, but on the other hand, we also need to arrest criminal activity such as depriving people of their Constitutional rights in favor of Islamic principles, e.g., beating women, honor killing, refusing to allow a woman to leave her home without a male escort, i.e., confinement. Many tenets in Sharia Law do not square with American Constitutional principles. Wives, for instance, are often treated more like property in this belief system and are often abused badly.

How do we deal with Sharia Law? Whenever one of these violations happens, arrest the perpetrator. Find the most serious statute violated and file multiple charges if committed. Failure to do so encourages further usurpations of our sovereign country.

Marxism, Socialism, and Communism

We will conclude our examination of worldviews with this continuum—Marxism to Communism—as it is surging in America right now. One has only to look at what is happening within our educational system today to understand why so many of those students seem to favor socialism. This section will be one of the shortest of my worldview examinations although it will probably be the one worldview that transforms America going forward. The reason I will keep this section relatively short is that this seems to be the one area that parents have now finally recognized. This is confirmed by the many heated school board meetings today.

I suspect that many public-school curriculums across the country will soon be returning to a more traditional fare rather than the currently developing CRT (critical race theory) curriculums and the like. One wonders, however, if this effort by parents has manifested soon enough or if the current number of socialistically-inclined Millennials and Gen Z voters represent a point of no return. A trigger point of sorts.

As for the police, these battles will largely be decided at the ballot box although there very well may be some very violent and large street demonstrations, vandalisms, and burnings similar to what we saw in Portland, Seattle, and Minneapolis in 2020 and what are beginning to manifest now against pro-life pregnancy centers and churches. We have already discussed woke rioters sufficiently elsewhere in this book, and what we need to do to prepare for those situations.

Truly, what we in law enforcement need to know about these people (socialists) is simply to recognize that they are everywhere. If they take to the streets the numbers could be huge and our preparation should include crowd control, riot training, gas dispersion, mass arrest techniques, and *many* new op-plans. The reality is that if these people keep their socialistic perspective over the next ten years, they will simply transform our country through the ballot box.

Recommendations: After researching and presenting a few of the mainstream worldviews such as utilitarianism, humanism, and the Judeo-Christian philosophies, in-service instructors should also present a few of the more exotic belief systems like Luciferian, Illuminati, and New Age beliefs to give some depth.

Instructing on these *Bad and Ugly* worldviews is to prepare officers for what they will be facing on the street in the near future. Things are becoming increasingly dark. The only way this is turned around is when we become points of light. If that sounds noble, it is!

Other Philosophies

An officer completing even a cursory Wikipedia investigation of worldviews for presenting an in-service training class on these philosophies will be impressed with the number of other worldviews that have been formalized into a "discipline" for explaining such questions as: ***Why am I here***; ***what is the meaning of life***; and ***do I count*****?** Even beyond their professional questions like, "Why am I doing this?" new policemen also ask these personal questions, thus the next chapter of this book. Many of the pagan philosophies today, like Hinduism, stress many gods with sometimes contradictory philosophies. This makes *finding "truth"* very difficult for ungrounded officers.

Wrapping Up Our Ethics Worldview Discussion

This chapter was opened by the title: "Worldviews, The Good, The Bad, and The Ugly." We then dove, head first, into some selfish worldviews and then into some evil ones, the Bad and the Ugly. Occultic practices can lead to "justifications" for doing some pretty horrendous things to our fellow humans, just look at Nazism in 1943-1945. Once these thought processes are generally accepted, anything is possible, including socialism, communism, and Nazism with its human genetic experimentation, super-race beliefs, euthanistic practices, and implementation of a "***Final Solution.***"

It is interesting that during the Nuremberg Trials, very little remorse was shown by convicted defendants for what they did *to their own citizens*. Not knowing what virtuous conduct entails will be a real problem in the future. Naïveté is not a good way to enter a profession like law enforcement, especially in this era. The big question for ending this chapter is: Will new officers be pillars of morality and strength for our citizens or will they be the S.S. of the New World Order? ❖

Chapter 12

Attributes of the Judeo-Christian Ethos

I do not want to continually drone on about this worldview or to say that there is nothing worthwhile in other worldviews for law enforcement, but I do think that the Judeo-Christian worldview is the motherload for good and great virtues necessary for good and great police officers, the gold standard so to speak. It is unquestionably the one on which this country was founded, and the one that carried it through more than 240 years of trials. It is not a carbon-copy of the biblical worldview, but it does share many attributes with that worldview.

Although I said that there may be elements in a few of the previously mentioned worldviews that are helpful for law enforcement in America, e.g., using "honest" science, employing good reasoning techniques, using the greatest good rationale, etc., the Judeo-Christian worldview has, in my opinion, the best self-contained set of attributes for **treating other people well** *while still* **accomplishing our law enforcement goals**. In this chapter, we will examine a few of the relevant virtues of the Judeo-Christian worldview that are important to police officers. We will then present a behavioral template based on the "chivalry" model that *can easily be used* in departments to foster the adoption of those virtues. And finally, we will offer a one-page listing of virtues at the end of this chapter that the author thinks important for officers.

The Judeo-Christian Worldview

For purposes of appealing to the widest audience, it is important that we first say that the Judeo-Christian worldview is not a religion! It is an ethos that has developed over thousands of years primarily out of two religions, but it is not a religious faith. That is important in this age of atheism. The fact is that statistics reveal that most Americans today who believe in this worldview are not orthodox Jews or true Christian believers. This worldview is a hybrid combination of *the values* shared by both religions, with many additional values that are not at all oriented towards religious practices. These values do, however, rely on a *single* deity to supply the laws of human interaction and conduct. **This is very important** for our evaluation of "truth."

These rules do not originate from man as many of the other philosophies do although man has certainly expanded on some of these. These rules are, consequently, independent of human cultural changes. A major principle from this viewpoint is that everyone will be responsible to God for their actions on earth at a "judgment" after death. This fact alone helps new officers in many ways. Many of the other worldviews believe that death ends it all or, like Islam, heaven must be earned by affirmative actions, like becoming a martyr. If one believes that death ends it all, anything you do here on earth, so long as you do not get caught doing the illegal things, is okay. After all, you are only here for a short time, so why shouldn't you attempt to get everything you can? This just makes good sense from that point of view.

American History 101: I mentioned early in this book that a mini-history course should now be presented to new officers in their basic training course. The subject matter of that mini-lesson should include the reality that America was built upon this worldview even though there have been many recent efforts (within the last five years) to disclaim America's Judeo-Christian foundation (note in particular the *1619 Project*). This is easily refuted by just a cursory review of quotations from the Founding Fathers, an examination of the "Great Awakening," and a reading of the Mayflower Compact and The Declaration of Independence. The Declaration, in particular, says that mankind has *inalienable rights* (meaning given by God and not by governments) which establishes a higher foundation for human government than just government or man himself.

Many of these Judeo-Christian principles for government were first codified in the Mayflower Compact—considered by some as our birth certificate as a country—years before the Constitution or the Declaration of Independence were written. This compact and other state (colony) constitutions undoubtedly influenced the writing of those later documents. We recently celebrated the 400th anniversary of the Mayflower Compact, written in November, 1620, which shows how long before 1776 that those principles were infused into our collective consciousness.

These principles are believed by many to be the reason for American exceptionalism as compared to the many other nations then moving out of a monarchy or empire-style government at about the same time as the American Revolution. By the way, "American exceptionalism" *does not* infer a hubris attitude. This term is worth googling. An interesting comparison—for those who want to see a pretty radical difference between two countries with a somewhat similar background—would be to do a quick-study of the French Revolution.

We opened this subject of the Judeo-Christian worldview with this short history of our country because it is so important today [Boy, I wish all of my history classes had been that brief]. My next statement will probably be a little surprising to my readers. After all of this hullabaloo about the Judeo-Christian worldview, I am going to present very few of the actual virtues (other than the "chivalry virtues") from this view. This is because these are so available, and I am not going to waste space in this "*Little Book*" on those when anyone can find these with a quick Internet search. In fact, an in-service class can and should be constructed presenting the virtues that are particularly important for law enforcement. So, let's get started in our examination of this remarkable worldview.

Why is the study of the Judeo-Christian worldview really worthwhile for officers in the 21st Century?

Perhaps the first important, although mostly unrecognized, reason for adopting this worldview is that it actually gives the officer more freedom. That really sounds counterintuitive. If an officer adopts this worldview as his primary worldview—and gives up his option of partially adhering to a hedonistic lifestyle some of the time, a utilitarian life view at other times, and a secular humanist view upon occasion—how can that actually lead to more freedom?

The truth is that accepting the Judeo-Christian worldview relieves a person from having to deduce, among many worldviews, attributes, and virtues which are important in this everchanging world with our many current cultural upheavals. Partially adhering to four or five worldviews is really having no worldview at all. An officer is constantly then afloat with no mooring.

One cannot truly "partially" adhere to a Judeo-Christian worldview when that worldview says there is only one determiner of moral correctness, John 14:6, Hebrews 13:8. One must either accept the "one determiner" principle or reject it. Knowing that the Judeo-Christian ethos comes from a monotheistic God gives some assurance that what this God says is correct. Manmade worldviews drift with culture. Officers need to know that there is truth (meaning a single standard) for moral conduct that verifies the nobility of their profession.

If one specifically adopts established standards, that person then knows what his limitations are. It is easier to adhere to standards—such as a noble (chivalrous) code of virtues, for example—when challenged by chaotic times if one *already* has a predetermined set of standards. This creates a strong foundation. A manmade standard in a secular humanistic worldview, for instance, may have seemed a really solid standard three years ago, but is no longer so. As an example, compare the principle of equality to equity. What a shift!

Knowing the simple fact that this country was founded on the Judeo-Christian ethos can lead officers to realize, perhaps for the first time, that this country is worth saving and serving, that their work is important, that there really is something known as American exceptionalism, and that there are still millions of citizens who adhere to these principles and appreciate their dedication.

The Benefits of Collegial Support: We have mentioned the many benefits of collegial support previously. Besides the direct benefit of adhering to a noble set of standards, officers will quickly recognize a side-benefit to adopting this ethos is the collegial support that adoption provides. This extends even beyond the department or the profession. With the Judeo-Christian worldview having been established for such a long period of time, it allows an adherent to be part of a broad collegial association rather than a cult.

Within the Judeo-Christian ethic, there are literally hundreds of religious denominations if one chooses to participate in one. For instance, one can adopt an evangelical worldview, a Catholic worldview, a Baptist worldview or any of a number of other worthwhile Christian worldviews which will provide a strong moral foundation and support for an officer. I will not even begin to discuss particular denominational characteristics because that has no result but to divide. All Judeo-Christian faiths provide huge benefits for officers even though there are many differences today among factions, even within the same denomination.

These differences sometimes appear great, but compared to worldviews like Marxism or secular humanism or an occultic worldview, they are small, much like the different denominations within our U.S. currency. There is a five-dollar denomination, a ten-dollar denomination, and a twenty-dollar denomination, but these are all U.S. currency, good for paying off a debt. In the 1950s, nearly everybody in America was singing off the same sheet of Judeo-Christian music, so to speak [maybe

I should have said, "so to sing"]. Not so today! The Judeo-Christian worldview has many competitors.

Recent Developments That Challenge: Having just said that denominational differences for law enforcement practitioners are not a real problem today, that may be changing in the future. The Pope has recently signed "an agreement of fraternity" with the high-ranking Grand Imams of al-Azher and also presented the agreement to the Buddhists, two very large religions. Many protestant churches have joined federations or aligned themselves under new "liberal" philosophies. Many other churches like the Lutherans and the Orthodox Christians are realigning with the Roman Catholic Church.

Unbeknownst to the average worshiper, we are today witnessing ecumenical unification—on an almost covert level—at warp speed. This sounds like a good thing, but as mentioned, this could, by design, lead to a single one-world religion that would **compromise** *all of the Judeo-Christian virtues*. That would be a bad thing, and it will eventually happen! My advice is to just monitor the situation and consider moving your affiliation to another denomination if the one you are in seems to be moving quickly into a one-world religious system.

It was not that long ago that such "agreements of fraternity" would have been unthinkable because of the huge doctrinal differences between Catholicism, Islam or Buddhism. These religions are just *so different*! Islam, for instance, does not believe in the Trinity. It believes that Jesus was a prophet but not the Son of God. Islam also believes that Jesus will come back in the end days, but he (the Islamic Jesus) will attempt to convert all Christians and Jews to Islam, and those who do not convert, he will kill. Christianity believes in moving towards peace and reconciliation (to an extreme, turn the other cheek). Islam believes in jihad and world domination (including lying to establish Islam, and war and chaos to hasten the coming of the Twelfth Imam). These foundational differences in dogma go on and on and are very profound, but these do not seem to be noticed at all today.

An Anchor: It is this author's opinion that it is time for those officers who do not have an anchor with a traditional belief system to find one, religious or otherwise, because of what is soon coming. Nearly all traditional religions will soon splinter, like the Methodist Church just did, separating the traditional faction from the highly progressive faction, but either of these is still better than having no established worldview. Just be aware of the one-world religion effort now taking place.

An Era of Oppression: We are moving into an era of tyranny and oppression, especially for those holding a Christian belief or adhering to the Judeo-Christian ethic, even here in America. European countries are well ahead of us in this respect with some believers already being criminally prosecuted for "hate crimes." All one needs to do is notice the attacks and burnings on churches and pro-life centers since the 2022 decision reversing *Roe v. Wade* to see the direction we are headed. Haven't heard about these attacks on U.S. churches? One must listen to nontraditional media sources to know about such things. We will reveal a few good nontraditional sources later in this chapter.

This tyranny and oppression, of course, involve more than just the religious element of society. Most are aware of the Left's attacks on free speech. This also involves the economic and governmental components of our society. The weakening or dissolution of America is not what we want to see as patriotic Americans, but it will be an eventuality, perhaps sooner than most think. How can that happen? Notice, the U.N.'s *2030 Agenda*, the World Economic Forum's (WEF's) Fourth Industrial Revolution, The Forum of Young Global Leaders movement, The W.H.O.'s agenda, The Green New Deal, etc. One of the most egregious is the U.N., in my opinion, because they were created to help maintain peace throughout the world. They have obviously been totally ineffective in this respect. Now, they say that the only way they can do this is to become the one-world governance body. Really!

We in law enforcement will not be able to change the course of history, but we can understand how we should handle these challenges, if prepared. As stated so often in this book, we can prepare for this, or we can be caught, again, off guard. Knowing what is coming is very comforting even if a little scary [there is my prophecy-perspective again]. Simply put, we can be a beacon of light or part of the problem. So, how do we become this beacon of light?

Building the "Chivalry Template"

What is this Chivalry Template that we claim will be helpful for officers? It is really a small sampling of virtues within the Judeo-Christian ethos that applies specifically to professions like law enforcement. It is an easy-to-remember, easy-to-use, set of rules for everyday employment. These virtues are those that most officers who answer a calling for this job [there is that calling thing again] have no problem in accepting.

We have mentioned that the use of a template—like what was professed in the legendary (perhaps mythical) King Arthur's Knights of the Roundtable story—can be helpful when officers today need support, direction, structure, and moral guidance. This legend has many inconsistencies in the supposed account. One big problem is that the legend was not documented (written down) until the 12th Century, allowing many years to tweak the legend, add personal interpretations, and omit important parts even if there was a shred of original truth. The ***template***, nonetheless, is ***very worthwhile*** for police officers in tumultuous times. So, what does this legend profess?

The Roundtable Account (Story, Legend, Myth) –

The province known in the Roman Empire as Britain was about equivalent in size to what we think of as the country of England today. Rome had controlled this area for many years before the first sacking of Rome occurred in AD 410. Most cite AD 476 as when the Western Roman Empire finally crumbled. Emperor Constantine had legalized the Christian religion in the empire in AD 313. Shortly thereafter the religion actually became the official religion in the empire. What a change this was, from burning Christians as street lamps and using them as lion food to becoming the official religion of the empire. Thereafter, if anyone wanted to advance in the Roman hierarchy, they really needed to become Christians, or at least act like they were Christians. How is any of this relevant today? Hold on. We are getting there.

The important point here is that as the empire was crumbling politically, the Christian religion had already been deeply infused into the system for over one hundred years. So, there was undoubtedly a deep-rooted Christian ethos present among those Roman leaders and soldiers in Britain. As those leaders in Britain realized that they were going to be less likely to be receiving support from Rome—meaning soldiers, weapons, new recruits, engineers, builders, clothing, supplies, money, skilled administrators, and the like—they needed to start shifting for themselves.

The new local system that they established would have likely had strong religious elements in it from the old Roman system, which would have at least made the "Roundtable legend" plausible and perhaps even probable, meaning that a new system would likely be steeped in the Christian virtues, thus the King Arthur story.

A Roundtable: This legend says that the Roundtable consisted of an order of knights dedicated to ensuring *the peace of Arthur* (the king's peace) throughout the realm. The knights were in fellowship with each other and the king, and each knight and the king had an equal right to speak at the table, thus a *round* table without a head position. The dictionary definition of chivalry defines their charge:

> **Chivalry** is the medieval knightly system with its religious, moral and social code. The combination of qualities expected of an ideal knight were ***especially*** **courage, honor, courtesy, justice** and **a readiness to help the weak.**

This indicates that a knight is also a champion of the ordinary man (the weak) even if he represents the king (the government), an interesting combination. The roundtable demonstrates the benefit and need for each officer (knight) to participate in the discussion, rather than disappearing into the ranks—remember the slogan: Leaders, lead—and the need to establish a *collegial relationship* (more than just a working relationship) with his fellow officers.

During the last few years, whenever I presented a promotion school, those courses really stressed how to facilitate a roundtable discussion and the benefits of using a roundtable format.

In our definition, the virtues specifically mentioned for knights are: courage, honor, courtesy, justice, and a readiness to help the weak. These—and a few other virtues that this author believes particularly important for modern-day officers—are listed at the end of this chapter. The Judeo-Christian ethos includes all of these, of course, as they actually came from that worldview (although that grouping of virtues was probably not labeled as the "Judeo-Christian" virtues in those days). What do these mean for our template?

Important Virtues for the Law Enforcement Profession in 2022, *AND* BEYOND!

The Chivalry Template: The first listed virtue is **courage**. Back in medieval days, physical confrontations with swords, daggers, and other hand weapons were common. Although we seem to be on a little higher level today, there are many indications that more aggressive times are afoot. Assaults on officers are rising as they did in the early 1970s (during the other time in our history that seems quite similar to today). Physical courage is the *outward* manifestation of valor, meaning bravery. I think this concept should not only be applied for our purposes to physical bravery in combat but also mental toughness and calmness when being challenged.

This template says that an officer must be **honorable** meaning he keeps his word. This has been discussed previously so we will not rehash those discussions.

An officer must be **courteous**. This concept is a little more vague and perhaps even more complex than most think. This is probably more like a super-gallantry concept when thinking about the times in which this gallantry concept developed. This is *more than just being respectful.* It is an apparent subordination to others—being humble—even though the officer is vested with much higher authority than the one to which he speaks, e.g., yes ma'am, no sir, may I inquire about ...

And finally, **justice**, meaning being evenhanded and balanced. We gave the simplest definition of an eye for an eye previously and some practical applications for officers. Perhaps the most important applications, for officers, are that they do not confuse justice with fairness, do not exhibit "equity" behaviors, or exercise partiality.

The last portion of the definition is self-explanatory: a readiness to help the weak. A whole mindset can be based on these terms, and hopefully will be.

This short explanation of chivalry can be fleshed-out at the department level, but it and the roundtable model can be used for many things including developing canons of conduct, proposing in-service training curriculums, and contributing ideas in certain management areas. A department chivalry template keeps officers thinking about what they *should* do. King Arthur may or may not have been a real person, but the benefits of building a template based on chivalry certainly has application today.

Some Alternative News Sources

In my listing of important virtues for law enforcement officers at the end of this chapter, I added the word "preparation" to the listing of virtues for the chivalry template. One must know what is coming to be able to prepare. There is very little argument that mainstream and social media today have corrupted themselves and become highly partisan. Consequently, officers need alternative news sources. I stress this again in this book because this is *so important*.

When I asked my promotion school officers in 2020 and 2021 who Klaus Schwab is and what the World Economic Forum and the Forum of Young Global Leaders do, **not one** officer in one class over those years had ever heard of these entities! Simply, by occasionally checking alternate news sources—like *The Epoch Times*, *Project Veritas*, *Citizen Free Press*, and one supposed "tin hat" source like *Prophecy Watchers* or *SkyWatchTV*—one's informational horizons will be greatly expanded. In September of 2022, the news begun to surface in a few mainstream news outlets that there are potentially some problems with the ingredients in the COVID shot. Those of us who watch non-legacy news outlets knew about these a year-and-a-half ago. A one-and-a-half-year gap is quite a span for supposedly "fast breaking" news outlets.

Summarizing the Judeo-Christian Mindset

On a personal level, officers—through training, becoming familiar with op-plans, via roundtable discussions or personal contemplation—must ponder potential, specific scenarios using the Judeo-Christian perspective before these present on the street, or they will likely exhibit immoral or unethical reactions when confronted with these new challenges.

On the macro-level, officers really only need to be somewhat aware of our moving towards a global government, economy, and religion to realize what is in store for them and where we are on the timeline.

They do not need to be *experts* in these areas, but *they do need to be aware of these*! Hopefully, I will never have another class in which no one knows who Klaus Schwab is or who Yuval Noah Harari is—our newest addition to the WEF—who talks openly and often now about "hackable humans" and other transhuman subjects. As diplomatically as I can relate this, his views of the near future are extreme, even by the radical Left's perceptions.

Virtues and Training: For those departments training officers who want to address these looming issues in in-service training, but cringe at thinking about the time and effort in preparing for such training, I am going to make a suggestion that will greatly reduce the effort needed for these classes.

Use this book as the seed material for your class and a roundtable discussion after your introductory lecture. Ask your class to read a chapter of this book and then discuss the material presented. In the following month, ask them to read another chapter and discuss that material after your lecture, and so on. One could easily formulate more than a year's worth of training in these critical areas by going chapter to chapter, month by month. Just something to think about.

In order to help prepare for these challenges, we have listed, below, a number of virtues, coming from the Judeo-Christian worldview, needed for flourishing in these difficult times. Yes, I used the word ***flourishing***! The darker it gets, the brighter the light seems. ❖

A Listing of Judeo-Christian Virtues Important to Law Enforcement

(The Chivalry Template)

Here is a one-page synopsis (starting point) for discussion on some of the virtues important for becoming a stellar police officer. Of course, accepting the Judeo-Christian ethic requires largely accepting the virtues and laws within that ethic: Thou shall not murder; Thou shall not steal, thou shall not bear false witness, etc., (the Ten Commandments, the Noahide Laws, and the more important New Testament axioms: be just, don't be a hypocrite, strive to be righteous, be a servant, be prepared to give your life for others, etc.). You can and should supplement this list as you see fit.

An Attitude of Service – The anti-hedonist virtue and view.

Selflessness – At a minimal level, recognizing that others have intrinsic value as human beings created in God's image.

Valor – Physical bravery AND the mental toughness to withstand the constant droning of anti-moralistic rhetoric and assaults in this modern society.

Honor – Keeping one's word.

Courtesy – Treating all well even when not treated well. More like gallantry.

A Preparedness Mentality – Training and planning for the events likely within the next couple of years that will be challenging for law enforcement. Keeping attuned to what destructive groups are planning.

Compassion – Not weakness nor dereliction of duty but a realization of what certain *kinds* of uncompassionate enforcement—e.g., immoral, draconian, or unconstitutional—will mean for America generally, its citizens, and the officer.

Grace – Undeserved mercy. Different than fairness which tends to diminish the culpability of a criminal act.

Discernment – This is an unusual virtue in that it typically requires some study and development rather than just merely accepting it. It is said that those who accept "the truth" in this time of planned deception can develop in this area much faster than others. It is separating the wheat from the chaff, the important from all the smoke and mirrors.

Wisdom – More than knowledge. Experience helps in this area. For our purposes, this involves knowing how to apply knowledge. Somewhat akin to discernment in that those who accept "the truth" can develop in this area much faster than others. Knowledge + experience + discernment = wisdom!

Chivalry – A framework, a template, upon which officers can build an honorable and successful career, as defined above.

Having now exposed these really bedrock virtues—yes, we have now circled clear back to the bedrock principles introduced at the very start of this book—we will next move into what we should actually do, specifically, within the department and then within the community with all that we have learned (and hopefully accepted).

Our shift here will be extreme, from the ambiguous and theoretical virtues to practical applications, but we have been preparing for these final steps ever since Chapter 1. Here is where the rubber meets the road. These final few steps will determine if we in law enforcement will become true professionals and a true profession! Our simple question to ponder for the end of this chapter is: Will we? ❖

Chapter 13

What to Do Next in the Department

So, is law enforcement in America a true profession today? Maybe. It is certainly very close in most states and actually may qualify as a true profession in certain departments. Nonetheless, even the best of the best can slip. Again, notice what happened within the FBI during the 2016 and 2020 elections, the lack of action in the 2020 riots, the hyper-actions of the January 6th riot, the lack of action in protecting churches and pro-life clinics after *Roe* was repealed, and the lack of action in protecting conservative Supreme Court justices. So, so sad! For the rest of our departments, the leap from occupation, skill, or art form to a true profession is probably not that far, and the time is now right, as they say, to make that leap.

In fact, if departments do not make that leap soon, they will likely miss that window of opportunity and be unprepared for what is to come. Unlike what happened in the 1960s, the federal government, universities, and states are not likely to jump in today. In short, the federal government is not likely to create new agencies like the *Law Enforcement Assistance Administration* or provide funding and expertise to help push us over the line. Colleges and universities are not likely to create new two- and four-year degree programs or new criminal justice certificate programs for law enforcement to help in this effort, and states are not likely to build new central academies for law enforcement in the immediate future. This time, the professionalization process will be mostly on us.

Seven Critical Issues for Local Departments

The Mechanical Elements: Many of the mechanical elements for a profession have already been accomplished in law enforcement. All states require successful completion of specialized training (an academy) and most states have a central continuing education requirement. Most states also have a decertification process for rule violations, and law enforcement now has a large number of professional journals currently in print. By and large, departments, academies and the profession have done well in this area.

Nevertheless, we still may have some weak areas that are, of course, not exactly the same across the country or across a state. It is up to individual departments to address those areas. Some departments, for instance, still allow applications from 18-year-olds. Maturity and life experience, especially several years of work experience, are more important today for officers than they have *ever* been. Although demanding a two-year degree of candidates has been counterproductive for some agencies, creating a tuition reimbursement program for tenured officers is a great alternative.

There are and will always be areas in which we debate what is really needed for officers. Nevertheless, there are some things that are clearly critical. So, here is a rundown of what we have identified as important for today (both in the mechanical and virtue areas):

1) The issue of answering a "**calling**" is really more than turning in an application and reporting for duty. Today, this should involve a good recruiting strategy. What personality traits should we be looking for? **Recruiting** has been a neglected area in recent years. Finding candidates who want *a career* and not just an interim job is critical. The second half of the recruiting question is developing

feeder-systems, like cadet programs and law enforcement "scouting" programs, and specialized certificate or associate degree programs that specifically prepare candidates for certain aspects of the occupation.

2) Most departments prefer to send recruits to a stress-academy. This is particularly important today. Nearly all academies put new officers through at least a **semi-stress environment** to see if these new officers can develop self-discipline, pay attention to detail under pressure, exercise good judgment while stressed, and handle technical legal issues in the heat of chaos. There has been a tendency over recent decades to minimize or do away with the stress element in an academy. This was and is a mistake. However, one danger of a stress academy is creating overly militarized departments. Nonetheless, some strategizing on this can create a system that largely avoids this problem.

3) **The Criticality of Virtue Training:** A department needs to develop ethical attributes it incorporates into canons of conduct, meaning a department Code of Professional Responsibility, a Declaration of Vision, at least one Mission Statement, and virtuous directives and policies. Then, as an absolutely necessary second tier to academy basic training, the department must provide training to new officers immediately after the academy on ethics, based on what is expected of them ***in that department*** because of their Mission Statement, directives, etc., which should culminate with a public oath or vow by those officers, incorporating these virtues, before friends, family, AND the media. Those ethical elements should not only be written in the above documents, but they should also be regularly acknowledged by the administration, encouraged, tested, trained, and rewarded in annual evaluations.

The Super-Secret Antidote – The Silver Bullet

When talking about virtues, there is always the argument—although not acknowledged publicly by most—that those who cut corners, cheat, or lie almost always seem to win. This gives them an unfair, sometimes insurmountable, advantage. I would have to say that this is often so. For officers, the same question also surfaces for them: why be virtuous? If one "fudges" a little on a search warrant affidavit, but then this results in finding evidence of a burglary that the suspect actually committed, why not? He actually is guilty. The officer is not, after all, attempting to convict him of a crime he did not commit. Is there anything the matter with a fishing expedition?

We, of course, mentioned several times earlier in this book that virtues are an inner commitment. American police officers adhere to virtuous standards because they individually commit themselves to those standards. It is a personal decision. There is no outside requirement of a good-for-a-good before they conform. Sometimes, however, this seems like a rather weak motivation. Here is a secret for when such deleterious thoughts creep in. This does not work every time but is a powerful truism. I call it the *Heroic Paradigm*.

Heroic Paradigm: There is something hardwired into us having to do with the heroic. People immediately recognize this and often want to follow or emulate those who exhibit this trait. This does not have to involve a death-defying event. It can be just standing firm for moral reasons when things seem stacked against us. It can be ***not*** fabricating information for a search warrant even if the bad guy is really, *really* a bad guy. Being the performer of a heroic act not only lets you recognize that you handled a situation morally—an important realization—but also inspires others to attempt to be more like you.

Two real-world macro examples of this are the two biggest building projects ever authorized for the Indiana Law Enforcement Academy. There have been less than five building projects authorized for that academy since the 1960s. The two biggest ***by far*** were in the 1960s and last year when the police were under attack—Defund the Police—but they continued to operate nobly all across the state.

In the 1960s, that legislation required a basic training program and then brought the academy out of the Indiana college system and built a beautiful academy complex with dorms on 313 acres of prime land just outside of Indianapolis. This past year, the legislature passed the largest appropriation for expansion of that academy since the 1960s. People, including legislators, are willing to close ranks with the police for a noble, heroic cause. I mentioned that states are not likely to just give us new academies, but at least in Indiana, when leaders, who had previously been seeking building and repair funds, year after year, are suddenly confronted by BLM and Antifa and Defund the Police movements, the unexpected can happen. Likewise, Queen Elizabeth II recently passed away. The viewership for her funeral (4.1 billion) was one of the largest ever. Flashy events like the Super Bowls draw a huge viewership (112 million in 2022) but quiet, determined, moral service is also recognized more than most think.

Why the heroic paradigm works, I have no idea. It is apparently a human character trait that God has instilled in each of us, i.e., admiration! Even though you did not send the bad guy to jail, this time, you set yourself apart as someone who follows the procedural rules rather than planting evidence or lying on an affidavit. As so often happens in this line of work, this will probably not be your only opportunity to send that bad guy away. Bad guys also seem to have a strong impulse to be bad guys—unless "saved." Your paths will probably cross again and again. Remember *The Heroic Paradigm* for big and small incidents. It is your silver bullet and will likely pay off for you and those watching you, eventually.

4.) **The Other Higher Elements:** All departments should include training in advanced writing skills within their in-service training as well as some training concerning our "American Constitutional republic" (our foundational concepts from history) and some advance legal training.

For the next several years especially, all departments should provide practical legal training on officer and department limitations concerning infringing on our **First Amendment** freedoms. That training should include those limitations as established by court decisions as well as department SOPs, Vision Statements, and canons of conduct. Depending on how things develop over the next year or two (meaning court decisions), the same type of training may be needed on **Second Amendment** issues. Unfortunately, the above suggested in-service curriculum is radically different than what most officers actually receive each year.

The Professional Skills – Annual in-service training curriculums typically involve firearms training, tactical search methods, defensive tactics training, driver training and the like. In all fairness, these subjects are, of course, high liability areas and should be trained, but the department must also mandate AND PROVIDE a second, higher layer of these other types of training. Only then will we begin to move into the area that most citizens consider the professional skills.

Local officers and administrators can certainly recognize what their particular departments need the most for handling current issues (think, roundtable discussions). Just recognizing these needs, however, is not the same as taking the next steps in this professionalization process. **Sir Isaac Newton** famously said that ***a body at rest tends to stay at rest***. Although meant to describe a principle in physics, we know that this maxim has other applications. The coronavirus and the 2020 riots very well may have a silver lining to them if we recognize this. That silver lining being the realization that **the time is now right** to take those last few steps towards professionalization.

5.) **One Important Issue is Discretion:** We mentioned a couple of times in this book that discretion is a big part of any true profession. Determining in what areas large amounts of discretion are worthwhile and in what areas guidelines need to be established is a difficult task. Law enforcement will always face dichotomies on discretion, i.e., being tough as nails at one end of the spectrum or being a teddy bear at the other end. Both of those extremes sound really bad, and they should! The true target is always somewhere in between, and it is constantly changing. Consequently, we will never satisfy everyone, but this does not mean we should just throw up our hands and do nothing.

If we decide to do nothing, we will find ourselves placing our officers in no-win situations that we know to be morally reprehensible. We will then likely double-down on that untenable position—into which ***we*** *have actually placed those officers* when an officer refuses to enforce that immoral or unconstitutional decree—by firing him.

Designing a Department Made for Millennials and Gen Z Officers

6.) We have moved into a period of time in which new recruits differ substantially from the Baby Boomer generation, upon which most training objectives were focused. One consequence of this shift is that it will take a substantially different approach to make Gen Z officers willing to stay on a department for an entire career. In the 1960s and 1970s, basic training academies were instituted, advanced training was available, and police discipline was designed around a society in which most candidates had prior military experience. The present law enforcement model and academy training approach have not changed much since those days.

Some areas that are now very different can be successfully addressed by local departments if these departments will just recognize these areas. An article by **Kimberlee Josephson** in ***The Epoch Times*** titled, "Why Job Turnover is So High for Gen Z and Millennials," 7/27/22, gives a concise listing of elements to consider. Here are a few that are particularly relevant for law enforcement.

She says, "Gen Z employees have had more structure and attention throughout their upbring than any other generation." In short, there has been a helicopter parent, teacher, or coach to tell them everything they should do and how to do it. That, unfortunately, is not a good formula for officers answering a hundred and one different kinds of calls.

Academy Focus: Academies should probably increase their scenario-based training to give more direction to recruits who have had very little "hard-knocks" experience. Such practical training may not have been as necessary in the 1960s or 1970s for prior military recruits but is much needed today. Academy training on the other end of the didactical spectrum should make law classes more demanding and writing skills more important.

Officer Needs: The Josephson article reveals that Gen Z workers **are very aware that they *are not* prepared** for the ambiguous, problem-solving, complex, creative, and communication demands (which I label as advanced writing skills) of their jobs. Doesn't each of these attributes sound like a highly important quality for a successful law enforcement career? These prior few paragraphs identify what new officers need for handling today's challenges, but also of importance is what they want.

Officer Wants – Work Satisfaction: Work satisfaction now rates as a high priority in their collective psyche. This may not have been such a high priority in previous generations. Today, if a new police employee experiences a rough patch or receives an offer of a higher paying job, that officer typically resigns from the department and moves on. What can we do to retain these people?

This suggests that we must actively create an environment in which the officer feels as if he is part of an important mission and profession. He wants to feel as if he is accomplishing something worthwhile. **Who am I? Why am I on this earth? Do I have a purpose? Do I count?** Satisfying these questions could potentially make a difference. Fostering collegial relationships could make a difference. An officer must also believe that he is accomplishing something noble and patriotic for the community and that this country is worth serving.

Good administrators can overcome all of these new challenges, but these are, in fact, *new* challenges, meaning that certain things will need to change. These are the important things that we have discussed in some detail already. There are other issues, of which we have only hinted, that should also be examined at staff meetings, roundtable discussions, and the like, a few of which are noted below (in the next section, just to get you started). Such roundtable discussions should be a regular occurrence in a Gen Z environment. Once we get started thinking along the lines of professionalism and preparation for the coming decade, those issues will surface for discussion naturally.

Minor Issues in the Professionalization Process

7) To begin to wrap up our discussion, we must admit that we also need to examine a number of minor issues. Some of these, although minor, really project a strong image to our citizens. One such minor area, highlighted here as an example, has to do with appearance and uniforms.

Appearancc and Uniform Choices: By the time this past decade (2010–2019) came to its completion, I noticed that normal duty uniforms in many local jurisdictions had gone in one of two directions, either golf-course casual with polo shirts, shorts, and tennis shoes (especially in the warmer climes) or completely tactical, with external bulletproof vests and shock plates.

If someone is on bike patrol, shorts, tennis shoes, and a polo-style shirt are certainly appropriate. Can casual uniforms, polo-style shirts, etc., become too casual? Perhaps. At the other extreme, there have also been repeated criticisms that the police have become an occupying military force. I think our use of tactical uniforms has significantly contributed to this. I realize that these uniforms are typically a popular choice by line officers. Nevertheless, the Robo-cop image is generally not a good thing for regular line officers.

I suppose, to a certain degree, that these tactical uniforms have become so common that the general public is no longer shocked by the presence of their "local military unit" patrolling their neighborhoods. Even more important, however, than what tactical uniforms project to citizens ***is the mindset it perpetuates within the officer***. One is as one dresses. The same might also be said of golf-course-casual uniforms. Can officers become so casual that they no longer command respect?

There are certainly specialty units and neighborhoods that require tactical or semi-tactical uniforms, but other areas ***may*** benefit from an officer wearing a Class A uniform. That concept has been discounted in many departments today.

As for a highly tactical mindset, civilian police forces were never meant to be an occupying military force. That image has probably contributed to the Defund the Police movement as well as other complaints about the police. In fact, a militarized police force was strongly discouraged *early on* (do a computer search on: the federal *Posse Comitatus* law that was ***passed in 1787***).

Even police departments need special permits to have fully automatic weapons, and police departments are not authorized to have weapons mounted on police helicopters or other police aerial vehicles. Likewise, military units cannot be housed within communities, in citizen homes, during peacetime, i.e., the U.S. Constitution, Amendment Three. This is because our Founding Fathers and Constitutional writers recognized that the presence of such forces within society ***dampens freedoms***! Police officers and police units can be highly abusive *within* *the law.* Law and Constitutional provisions provide only the outer limits for conduct. Not every abusive police tactic can be—or should be—prohibited within the Constitution. A police department being self-limiting and disciplined is truly a sign of a professional department.

Light-years of Progress

The truth is that we have come light-years professionally from the early 1960s. This is not obvious to many since they were not around then to see the difference now. Nonetheless, we may need to take another step or two to plant our feet squarely on true bedrock. These final few steps are very attainable and are much easier than many believe if we can just shed that stubborn mindset that *we are just fine the way we are.*

In fact, these final steps can be publicized, by a good chief, to highlight to our citizens that the *department officers* are leading the way in creating a professional department (very good PR). Just like a forest floor or a Kansas plain, the ground is best for regrowth after a fire. We in law enforcement have already experienced much of that fire. This time of confrontation and turmoil may produce some fertile ground for growing a great department and profession! Let us not waste it! ❖

Chapter 14

What to Do Next in the Community

For all of you reading this, citizens and officers, who took the time to consider the concepts presented in *The Little Blue Book on Police Ethics*, I thank you! I wrote this because I believe strongly that the time is now right to generate the momentum and to gain the support for professionalizing all of those who protect us. There are now politically correct reasons for both officers and commanders—and for even the most liberal councilmen and councilwomen—to proceed with this effort. There is a saying among revolutionaries: Never waste a crisis! The bad guys *always* seem to use this principle. Why not the good guys?

Our officers need our support for these final few steps. Some of these next-steps will take a modest amount of financing but most involve little more than focus and will. As one who has closely watched and participated in the law enforcement system since the 1960s, I have seen huge improvements as well as several swings in attitudes over the years. I did not have a family history or personal experience that led me to law enforcement. In fact, my dad thought all officers took the job so that they could be "on the dole!" My employment was a calling in the purest sense of the word.

As an impressionable boy in the early 1950s, when my family lived in the deep south, I remember hearing from my parents that Annie, our African-American housekeeper, would not be coming to work one day as she had gotten arrested by the police for vagrancy. I also remember my parents saying that she was the hardest working lady that they had met, and she was certainly not a vagrant. She worked at a different house on our block each day.

When I took my first criminal justice class in the late 1960s, the cities were erupting in violence after Dr. Martin Luther King Jr. was assassinated. I saw the police on TV, confronting peaceful demonstrators, with dogs and with high pressure water hoses. I remember the television coverage of the Ohio National Guard shooting down several college demonstrators. I remember thinking to myself that a different city would likely burn each night.

It was shortly thereafter that something wonderful started to happen within the police ranks. Some officers started to view themselves as professionals. I know because I signed up for the MP Corps in early 1971 when these things were happening. There was a lot of support and a lot of money for these changes in those days. One thing that I noticed which may or may not be an indicator (or a real link) to the professionalization process was that nearly all city police cars in the 1950s were painted black and white. By the 1970s, city police cars had numerous color schemes and flashy new decal designs. To me, this signified the new, more open (dare I say, progressive) mindset within law enforcement.

With the new basic training requirement and, a little later, the in-service training requirements, the technical competence of law enforcement officers exploded. In those days, a black and white cruiser was not to be found. Then came 9/11 in 2001. Thereafter, I noticed police uniforms everywhere changing from the typical Class A or Class B (dress) uniform to the BDU style uniform. We were becoming domestic military units, and much to my dismay, I began seeing a large number of black and white cruisers again.

As previously mentioned, when I started at the academy as a full-time staff instructor in 1986, our basic training classes were about 60 to 80 officers. This was well within our training capabilities. By the time

I retired in 2017, our class enrollments were capped at 170 officers (because this was the largest classroom we had) and there was a long waiting list for each class. The number of full-time certified officers in the state had changed very little. We were just not retaining officers.

Along this line, I spoke with the sheriff from my home country at one of our graduation ceremonies just before I retired. He said that they have had five vacancies that they have been attempting to fill for years. As soon as they hire someone and send that person to the academy, one or two others quit, and they cannot catch up. I later found that even the officer graduating that day did not make it past the probationary period.

Council members could establish a tuition reimbursement program for officers who are taking college classes in a criminal justice or related area. Although this might sound expensive, it will likely help retain officers for the long run. It is high turnover rates that are truly budget busters. Anyone familiar with the process knows that screening and training new officers is *extremely* expensive. Any step taken to retain officers is worthwhile. Likewise, having a very young department also has some real ramifications in how calls are handled.

Similarly, establishing a feeder-system was and would likely again be worthwhile. Sponsoring a law enforcement "scouting" troop or creating a cadet program seems an effort whose time has again come. Applicants from these groups *actually know what is expected of an officer* after they have served as cadets for a couple of years. They have had time to develop the proper mindset to complete a 20-year career, and department officers are already familiar with a cadet-applicant when he turns in his application on his twenty-first birthday.

I also mentioned that chiefs should encourage roundtable discussions. These roundtable discussions should identify areas needing work in the department as a first step. Then community leaders and the mayor should be included in the roundtable discussion. Next, key council members should be included. Finally, credit should be given *publicly* to the officers who got a particular process started to ensure future participation.

In late 2019, nearly everyone would have said, if asked, that the likelihood would be slim to none if an officer put his knee on an arrestee's neck that this would spark multiple months and then years of demonstrations, rioting, burnings, and calls to defund all police departments. Likewise, who would have thought then that the police would be enforcing broad emergency decrees in which they would be accused of constitutional violations, over-reactions and abuse? These are the reasons that these canons of conduct should be among the first things attempted in roundtable discussions that involve the community and council. We now have a generation that truly believes in socialism and that the police are brutal and that the world is racist. This will take *decades* to change, but we can make changes within our departments in a relatively short period of time.

And finally, the community, council, mayor, and merit commission should continue to keep pressure on the department to initiate and continue a second, higher level of training in their in-service training programs including advanced writing skills, ethics studies, mentoring skills and the like. In the police skills, interviewing techniques, statement analysis, body language, and crime prevention classes fit into these advanced criteria. So too with specialty areas like management, K-9, and armorer's classes.

There are so many higher-level classes available that a chief should never be at a loss for finding a focus area for a particular year, and more importantly, council members should be receptive to funding these areas. Most of these are not hugely expensive. Keeping shooting skills finely honed is, of course, important, but those types of manual skills are truly blue collar. We need to train in higher skills and in more areas than hand-to-hand combat.

One of the most famous change-agents of the nineteenth century was Frederick Douglas. I quoted him at the beginning of this book. While he was talking about freedom—to make my case for a new and improved law enforcement system—I would use his insightful observations here by substituting the words "*Those who want a true profession*" for his words of "*Those who profess to favor freedom*." Douglas said,

"Those who profess to favor freedom and yet depreciate agitation, are people who want crops without ploughing the ground; they want rain without thunder and lightning; they want the ocean without the roar of its many waters. The struggle may be a moral one, or it may be a physical one, or it may be both. But it must be a struggle. Power concedes nothing without a demand. It never did and it never will."

Blessed are the peacekeepers and those who battle for improvement. ❖

Michael J. Lindsay
LETB & ILEA Deputy Director (retired)

Postscript

This book was written to bring officers quickly up to speed on what is happening in the world. It dives deeply into actual end-time prophecies without dwelling on these or getting "churchy." It aligns real-world events with these prophecies—current to within days of when this work was submitted to the publisher—and convincingly shows what is next.

If a reader wishes more information on any of these seemingly never-ending catastrophes and the prophecies that predict these things from more than 1900 years ago, Mike's other books nicely supplement this work. Each has a prophetic subplot that educates. In fact, completing any one of Mike's books will likely place the reader at a point well ahead of ninety percent of senior pastors in the area of end-of-the-age prophecy. All of Mike's books are short and easy to digest with chapters that lend themselves to one-a-day readings.

This book's structure is designed to answer the many questions surfacing today as well as the shrouded events likely to begin surfacing during the fall festivals (September and October). Not surprisingly, one attribute of human nature is that people will attempt to avoid unpleasant situations until these circumstances inescapably manifest in their lives. Police officers need a leg up on these events. Mike Lindsay's books are all designed to clear the fog and unpack the deceptions of these latter-day events. One can find his other works by searching his name, Michael J. Lindsay, on Amazon.com. You can also read his blog at: https://thetowncrierreports.wordpress.com

About the Author

Michael Lindsay was a 46 plus-year law enforcement officer and administrator. He began his career in 1971 as an MP in the Army during the Vietnam era and was eventually charged with establishing a military police investigation unit at his permanent duty station in Kansas. Upon completing this task, he was awarded the U.S. Army Certificate of Achievement and promoted to sergeant.

After completing his military obligation, Mike returned to civilian life where he worked as a deputy marshal, park policeman, and special deputy while completing his A.S. and B.S. degrees in criminal justice as well as two terms of a law degree before marrying his sweetheart, Denise, in 1980. Upon embarking on his career after his marriage, he was offered the marshal position in Westville, Indiana, where he previously served as a deputy. He held the chief marshal position for nearly seven years at that department. He then accepted a full-time staff instructor position at the Indiana Law Enforcement Academy (ILEA) in 1986.

Mike later moved to Arizona and taught several criminal justice subjects in the community college system there. In 2003, he took employment with the US Marshal Service (Air Operations) transporting prisoners across the western United States and to El Salvador, Guatemala, and Honduras.

In 2006, Mike was called back to ILEA as the Deputy Director for the Law Enforcement Training Board and academy. He held that position until he retired in October of 2017, after 46½ years of active law enforcement service. Mike then began writing and presenting police promotion schools before becoming a full-time author in 2021. Mike has had two previous books published, and he self-published one other. He is a graduate of several professional schools and courses including two death investigation schools and the FBI National Academy.

Just before his retirement, Mike discovered Bible prophecy and has been amazed by it ever since. ❖

Yellowstone National Park
March 5, 2019

Endnotes

All endnotes are from Chapter 1

Endnotes

1 Matthew 24:4, deception

2 The New American Standard Edition uses the words "birth pangs." Other versions use the word "sorrows."

3 Matthew 24:34, this generation shall not pass away

4 Psalm 90:10, a generation is 70-80 years

5 "Only 6% Of Americans Believe Biblical Worldview, Barna Survey Reveals"

https://www.christianitydaily.com/articles/11996/20210527/only-6-percent-of-americans-believe-biblical-worldview-barna-survey-reveals-family-research-council.htm

6 "Democrats File New Bill Authorizing 'Strike Force' to Imprison Unjabbed Families: 'Our Internment Camps Are Ready'" [state of Washington]

https://apps.leg.wa.gov/WAC/default.aspx?cite=246-100-040

7 "New York declares COVID state of emergency as governments across globe race omicron variant"

8 "Night of Broken Glass," November 9, 1938

https://www.history.com/topics/holocaust/kristallnacht

9 COVID-19: Democratic Voters Support Harsh Measurer Against Unvaccinated. [1/12/2022]

https://www.rasmussenreports.com/public_content/politics/partner_surveys/jan_2022/covid_19_democratic_voters_support_harsh_measures_against_unvaccinated

10 Revelation 6:6-8, inflation, and food shortage (also known as the Four Horsemen of the Apocalypse)

Lightning Source UK Ltd.
Milton Keynes UK
UKHW020802230123
415815UK00015B/437

9 781662 865121